MARCRAFT INTERNATIONAL CORPORATION

Train with the Pros!™

NETWORK +
CERTIFICATION
LAB GUIDE

Editor in Chief: Stephen Helba
Assistant Vice President and Publisher: Charles E. Stewart, Jr.
Production Editor: Alexandrina Benedicto Wolf
Design Coordinator: Diane Ernsberger
Cover Designer: Michael R. Hall
Cover Art: Michael R. Hall
Illustrations: Michael R. Hall and Cathy J. Boulay
Production Manager: Matthew Ottenweller

This book was set in Times New Roman and Arial by Cathy J. Boulay, Marcraft International, Inc. It was printed and bound by R.R. Donnelley & Sons Company. The cover was printed by Phoenix Color Corp.

Pearson Education Ltd., *London*
Pearson Education Australia Pty. Limited, *Sydney*
Pearson Education Singapore, Pte. Ltd.
Pearson Education North Asia Ltd., *Hong Kong*
Pearson Education Canada, Ltd., *Toronto*
Pearson Educación de Mexico, S.A. de C.V.
Pearson Education–Japan, *Tokyo*
Pearson Education Malaysia, Pte. Ltd.
Pearson Education, *Upper Saddle River, New Jersey*

Written and edited by: Randy Ratliff, Caleb Sarka, Evan Samaritano, Wanda Dawson, and Bradon Kanyid

Earlier editions by Marcraft International Corporation: 2000 and 1999.

10 9 8 7 6 5 4 3 2 1

ISBN 0-13-060627-8

TRADEMARK ACKNOWLEDGMENTS

All brand and product names are trademarks or registered trademarks of their respective companies. All terms mentioned in this book that are known to be trademarks or service marks are listed below. MARCRAFT cannot attest to the accuracy of this information. Use of a term in this book should not be regarded as affecting the validity of any trademark or service mark.

MS-DOS is a registered trademark of Microsoft Corporation.

Windows, NT, Millennium, 2000, 95, 98, Office, Word, and Windows for Workgroups are registered trademarks of Microsoft Corporation.

MARCRAFT is a registered trademark of Marcraft International Corporation.

CISCO, and its referenced products, are registered trademarks of CISCO Systems.

Cabletron, and its referenced products, are registered trademarks of Cabletron Systems Incorporated.

Rockwell, and its referenced products, are registered trademarks of Rockwell Corporation.

NetWare, Novell, and Novell Client are registered trademarks of Novell Incorporated.

FEDERAL COMMUNICATION COMMISSION NOTICE

This equipment generates and uses radio frequency energy, which may cause interference to radio and TV reception if it is not installed and used according to the manufacturer's instructions. This equipment has been tested and found to comply with the limits for a Class B computing device, in accordance with FCC specifications in Subpart J, Part 15. These specifications are designed to provide reasonable protection against radio frequency interference in a residential installation.

However, there is no guarantee that interference will not occur in a particular installation. If this equipment does cause interference to radio or television reception, which can be determined by turning the equipment off and on, the user is encouraged to try and correct the interference by one or more of the following measures:

Reorient the receiving antenna.

Relocate the computer/modem with respect to the receiver.

Move the computer/modem away from the receiver.

Ensure that the expansion slot covers are in place when no option board is installed.

Use properly shielded cables and connectors.

Plug the computer/modem into a different outlet so that the computer and the receiver are on different branch circuits.

If necessary, the user should consult the dealer, or an experienced radio/television technician, for additional suggestions. The user may find the following booklet prepared by the Federal Communications Commission helpful: "How to Identify and Resolve Radio-TV Interference Problems."

This booklet is available from the U.S. Government Printing Office, Washington, D.C. 20402. Refer to Stock No. 004-000-00345-4 when ordering this booklet.

Table of Contents

Creating Standard Operating Procedures

OBJECTIVES

1. Determine the minimum fields required in a standard operating procedure (SOP).
2. Create a template for a SOP.
3. Write SOPs related to controlling network documentation, operation, and maintenance.

Planning Strategy

RESOURCES

1. Network+ Certification Training Guide
2. Windows 2000 Professional workstation with a word processor installed

DISCUSSION

As computer networks grow in complexity and as business decisions revolve around their contributions to a company, a consistent approach to networking has become a requirement. Documenting key areas of a network is an effective way to ensure that the network remains a contributor to an organization's success, and not a deterrent.

A network is a complex process affected by many attributes of the process—the user, equipment installed, cabling infrastructure, software installed, level of maintenance, basic design, cost controls, and so on. The list is as large as many of the networks in use today. And these, in terms of size, may be limited to a single room or they may span the globe.

In managing a complex process—no matter if it's automation in a factory, a sales force, purchasing, maintenance, or computer networks—the end goal is to continuously improve the process. The only way to do that is to begin with a known baseline, compare actual results against the baseline, then implement changes that will drive improvements. The conventional way of beginning is to document the system.

Documentation comes in many forms. It may be nothing more than scribbled notes passed from user to user that list steps on how to do an operation, or it may be a formal procedure that's subjected to various levels of review and approval before being released. At times, the documentation is a drawing that shows, for example, how to connect peripherals to a computer or how to fit a cable with an end connector. Other times, it may consist of electrical parameters such as voltages, frequencies, or the shape of waveforms used to troubleshoot a circuit card. Regardless of the level of formality of documentation, several characteristics should be insisted upon in order to preserve the integrity of a goal of continuous improvements. These include:

- Unique Title
- Revision Control
- Approval
- Controlled Distribution

Typically, in a documentation system, these characteristics are placed in the header of a document template that all personnel involved in writing and developing procedures must follow.

A unique title may seem insignificant until you consider that the trend in user documentation is toward paperless systems. Consider the help menu used with computer software. You can search the help database for keywords or scan a list of titles for subject matter relevancy. To do so, the titles listed must be unique. The same is true of a group of networking procedures that are placed on a network. The user may begin with an index or table of contents, click on a title, and be connected to that procedure. Again, in order to be effective, the titles must be unique.

There's another reason to make all standard operating procedures unique. If two procedures share an identical title, how will a network user—one less informed than yourself—know which is the one they want? There's a risk they may follow the steps in the wrong procedure.

Revision controls represent fundamentally good business. Recall that a documented system is begun as a baseline effort. If the system is audited for compliance and usefulness, there will be invariable changes; changes that will improve the system. As each change is implemented, the revision control increments. For example, assume you're working on a printed circuit board and have a list of relevant voltages that were compiled from a known-good board. If the manufacturer of the board makes a hardware change, the voltages may change. However, if you're troubleshooting with the list of old voltages, you'll be using obsolete data to find the problem.

By instituting revision controls of the documentation you're using, you will always know if you're using the latest and most current data in your job. The usual method is to compare the revision level of the document you're using to a controlled revision list of documents.

The problem is compounded with advances in software upgrades for circuit boards. A manufacturer releases upgrades designed to fix problems in a product. Before installing an upgrade, you must know the current version of the software as well as the version installed in the board.

There are many ways to implement revision-control. The simplest is to date-control a document. This means that each document contains a date representing the most current version of the procedure. You compare the date of a document to a master list that includes the most current dates of all documents. If the date on the list exceeds the date of the document you're using, then your document is obsolete.

An approval is necessary to ensure that a procedure is representative of the desired outcome. For example, you may write a procedure that specifies how a user is to notify network support of a problem. A user could write the same procedure differently, as well as anyone else who ever needs to contact network support. But as the manager of a network, you recognize that certain steps, historically, have worked in resolving problems. This is the approach you want all users to use. Consequently, you approve a procedure that only lists these steps, and expect everyone else to reference it before contacting network support.

An approval process ensures consistency. When followed, it helps to create a baseline for conducting business since everyone will be using it as a reference. This isn't to say that an approved procedure is the best approach, but it is an effective means of analyzing changes before they're implemented to ensure that they make sense and will, in fact, be an improvement.

Controlled distribution means that only approved SOPs will be publicly released. Normally, anyone in an organization can change, or write, a procedure and submit it for approval. Those individuals tasked with reviewing the procedure will either approve or disapprove the document. If approved, the master list is updated, the revision control incremented, and the document distributed. In this way, distribution is controlled and there's a sense that only relevant and current documents will be used.

Creating standard operating procedures isn't on the list of favorite things to do of most networking personnel. However, it's become a critical component of their jobs since a company's network has a dramatic effect on its success. CompTIA recognizes the importance of SOPs in their Network+ Certification testing. Based on a wide-ranging survey of the industry, they recommend, at a minimum, the networking titles listed in Figure 1-1.

CompTIA List of Recommended Networking SOP Titles	
How to Configure Network Software	Problem Escalation Protocol
SOP for Disaster Recovery	Distribution of Controlled Documents
Troubleshooting Flowcharts	How to Identify a Problem
Cable Labeling Conventions	Revision Control of Controlled Documents (SOPs)
How to Document System Changes	Strategic Plan for Growth and Capacity
SOP for Internal and External Security	How to Back Up Server Data
System Floorplans	How to Set Up Peripherals
How to Set Up User Accounts	How to Set Up a Server
Service Contracts-Information About, and Locations	How to Set Up Clients
How to Change User Accounts	Establishing Testing Standards and Benchmarks
Format for Controlled Documents (SOPs)	Format for Creating Controlled Documents

Figure 1-1: Networking SOPs as Recommended by CompTIA

In this Lab Procedure, you'll create a template for a controlled document, then write an SOP.

PROCEDURE

Planning Strategy

Figure 1-2 shows a template for a controlled SOP. It contains the fields described in the previous discussion along with several others. While there are no specific rights and wrongs to writing SOPs, the fields listed in the figure are typical of most controlled documents. Formats vary from company to company, but they all share—or should share—those minimum fields as previously described.

The Revision field in the template is separate from the Date field. As indicated in Figure 1-2, the Date is used to specify the date the document was released to the public. The revision may be any assortment of alphanumeric designations with the simplest system consisting of a letter, such as Rev A. Other systems call for a dotted decimal number, such as 1.0. Minor changes cause the level to increment to 1.1, 1.2, and so forth. A major change to the document will cause the level to increment from 1.x to 2.x.

Whatever type of revision control you work with, make sure that anyone who uses the documents understands the control so they can verify the currency of the documents they're referencing.

The Revision History is often a required field because it prevents duplications of past changes. The history is normally dated and a brief description included that summarizes the change. In some types of document control systems, the Revision History references users to another document that contains detailed changes made to a document.

The fields shown in Figure 1-2 from COMPANY NAME, down to DISTRIBUTION LIST, are usually placed in the header of a document template. The template is then made available to anyone wanting to create a procedure. By specifying the required fields, a level of consistency is maintained from document to document.

COMPANY NAME	
TITLE: *Titles must be unique, and be referenced by a master list of titles.*	
REVISION: *Revision levels may be alphanumeric.*	DATE: *The date is normally the date on which the approved procedure was released.*
APPROVALS: *Approvals include management, supervisors or engineers.*	
REVISION HISTORY: *This is a listing of previous revisions, and a brief description of the change that caused the revision level to increment.*	
DISTRIBUTION LIST: *This is a list of physical locations (or individuals) where an approved and current copy of the relevant SOP can be found.*	
SCOPE AND OBJECTIVE	*Scope refers to who (group, individual, department, etc.) the procedure applies to.* *Objective refers to the desired outcome of the procedure.*
PROCEDURE	*This is where, stated as simply and clearly as possible, the specific steps or requirements that must be followed are given. Following these steps should achieve the objective of the procedure.*
RELEVANT PROCEDURES, FORMS, AND MANUALS	*If another procedure, vendor manual, or required form is relevant, it should be listed here.*

Figure 1-2: Format for a Standard Operating Procedure

The body of the procedure contains a Scope and Objective field. These two items are sometimes combined into a single entry called Purpose. No matter the title, one of the first entries in the body of a procedure will be to describe why the SOP exists. Figure 1-3 shows an example of a Scope and Objective statement.

SCOPE AND OBJECTIVE	*This procedure applies to all employees with e-mail access. It specifies cc:mail as the only e-mail tool permitted, and describes how to send and receive e-mail with cc:mail.*

Figure 1-3: Objective/Scope or Purpose Statement

Notice that the reader is told in the beginning who the procedure applies to and what it will accomplish.

The Procedure section of the SOP contains step-by-step instructions. Figure 1-4 is a sample of the Procedure section:

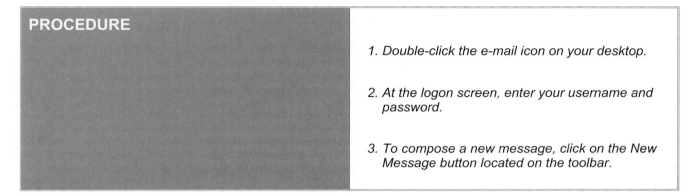

PROCEDURE	1. *Double-click the e-mail icon on your desktop.*
	2. *At the logon screen, enter your username and password.*
	3. *To compose a new message, click on the New Message button located on the toolbar.*

Figure 1-4: Procedure Section

Notice that sentences are kept short and only contain information the user needs. Some procedures will include illustrations to help the reader better visualize the steps required to perform a task. In this sample, the cc:mail toolbar can be seen by clicking the underlined word "toolbar" in the sentence in the right column. This approach has the advantage that the procedure isn't cluttered with graphics that may take time to load and won't be pertinent to all users.

The procedure continues until all steps are written that satisfy the purpose of the procedure. You may need to include other fields depending on the SOP. If specialized equipment or tools are needed, include a heading in the left column called Equipment. If there are vendor manuals or CDs containing additional information that would be helpful, include a heading called Reference Materials. Safety may be a concern and if so, include a Safety heading that specifies precautions, emergency shutdown procedures, etc.

The best way to get a feel for writing procedures is to write one. But before doing so, create a template to use for other procedures you'll be writing in the course of these Lab Procedures.

1.	Using a higher end word processor such as Microsoft Word or Corel WordPerfect, create a template for a procedure by using Figure 1-2 as a pattern.

2.	Use the Table tool to create the header fields as well as the columns in the body of the document.

3.	Once you've finished the template, save it using the file name **procedure.wpt** (for WordPerfect) or **procedure.dot** (for Word).

This template can be used over and over as you create controlled documents. We'll begin by writing a procedure in which you specify the format of all SOPs.

The header of the procedure is to include the following:

COMPANY NAME: *Your full name*

TITLE: *Format For Creating SOPs*

REVISION: *A*

DATE: *The date you write the procedure.*

APPROVALS: *Network Administrator, Operations Manager, Documentation Supervisor*

DISTRIBUTION LIST: *Network Support, Production, Sales, Documentation, MIS, Shipping and Receiving, Purchasing, Training*

4. Next, write a Scope and Objective statement.

5. Write the body of the procedure. Specify that all SOPs must use the template and include a brief explanation of all fields. Feel free to include any information that you believe will be relevant to someone writing a SOP.

6. Once you're finished, have your instructor review the final document.

Feedback

LAB QUESTIONS

1. Why should an SOP include revision controls?
2. Why should the header of an SOP include a field for approvals?
3. Why is it important to include a field specifying the distribution list?
4. Create a standard operating procedure titled *Distribution of Controlled SOPs*. Refer to the information presented in this Lab, then specify a method that all users are to follow when submitting new or changed SOPs, approval systems, or release and control of approved documents.

Creating a Network Floorplan

Planning Strategy

OBJECTIVES

1. Determine cabling needs and runways for a typical office.
2. Properly locate PCs and cable runs to avoid interference.
3. Label all entry and exit points of the cable run.
4. Plan for future growth and changes.
5. Write standard operating procedures for a cable install and for labeling connections.

RESOURCES

1. Network+ Certification Training Guide
2. Cabling specifications and characteristics
3. Standard Operating Procedure template

DISCUSSION

Network documentation has increasingly become an important part of a network administrator's job. This is because not only have users become more sophisticated and, therefore, prone to taking risks with the technology at their disposal, but the effective operation of a complex network relies on the proper operation of many components.

Documenting how the pieces are to fit together is critical to the continuing reliability of a network. We're particularly reliant on networks as a business tool, as a means of personal communication, as a research tool, as a marketing tool, and as a product development tool. More and more, companies rely on the Internet as a means of reducing costs and serving customer needs. For example, software (or firmware) upgrades are routinely made available as downloads from the vendor's web site. Upgrades usually contain fixes to bugs not resolved before a product was released to market, so timely access to them is important.

But when should an upgrade be installed once it's available? Who should do the install? What if the upgrade creates more problems than it fixes? What if it interferes with other software running on a network? Should all users receive the upgrade? While rather elementary questions, they're important since any of them, if the wrong decision is made, can have adverse effects on the user's ability to perform his/her job.

In this procedure, you'll develop a standard operating procedure (SOP) that specifies how to lay out and label the cabling for a small local area network. The format you'll use contains those elements most commonly used for controlled documentation. "Controlled," in this context, means that any changes made to the SOP must be duly approved in a formalized manner. The documentation department of a company will have procedures that detail how a procedure can be changed and the steps required to have it approved and redistributed.

Why should there be formal steps to changing a procedure, a step-by-step process for submitting changes, and a method for approvals and redistribution? Because it imposes consistency on a network, and on any process that must be placed in a state of controls in order to work at peak efficiency. In most cases, procedures are periodically audited to determine whether they're being followed. If they are, fine. If they aren't, it may mean that the user/network operator isn't doing his/her job; or it may mean that the same user/network operator is doing something better than is documented in the procedure. If so, an audit will reveal an opportunity for improvement that otherwise wouldn't have been implemented on a wide scale.

In the following procedure, choose a cabling media, then sketch an installation onto a floorplan that includes properly located computers and a workable cable labeling scheme. Once you've finished, you'll develop SOPs that describe the layout of a network, and how to label each connection in the network.

Planning Strategy

PROCEDURE

Cabling issues are often the greatest problem for network technicians. Ideally, the cable scheme used in a network is meticulously documented, the cable type used in the network is consistent throughout the network, and future growth has been addressed. But in the worst case, you may find yourself responsible for a network in which none of the above has been done.

An illustration showing a floorplan is depicted in Figure 2-1. The dotted line squares in each of the offices represent the location of fluorescent lights. Fluorescent lighting is often a source of unacceptable noise for twisted pair installations. An elevator shaft and maintenance department have been included in the figure as well because they are common sources of interference.

Within this lab, we'll first develop a floorplan for Figure 2-1 that addresses electrical noise. The floor plan will have properly documented cable runs and connections, and allow for future growth. For our example, we will use a bus topology connected by twisted pair cabling. Twisted pairs are identical to the wire in your home that runs to the telephone.

When developing a floorplan, the location of walls and all possible sources of interference such as motors, generators, fluorescent lights and any type of heavy machinery should be included. Once the floor plan has been sketched, you must decide where the cables will run—behind the walls, behind the baseboards, above the ceiling, or, in some cases, under the floor.

Figure 2-2 lists several guidelines that will serve as an aid for planning an installation. In addition, Figure 2-3 lists pertinent data about various cable types that will be helpful when planning an installation.

A possible arrangement for installing a network onto the floor of Figure 2-1(a) is shown in Figure 2-1(b). Note that the network cable runs through the ceiling and down the walls to a tap box. Several observations can be made from the figure. The computers have been located along the walls at a central point in the offices. This provides flexibility if the occupant of the office decides to engage in a bit of interior redecorating.

All PCs have been located on the outside wall, which is the farthest distance from the heavy-duty motors associated with the elevator. Likewise, the PCs in the machine shop have been located the farthest distance from the compressor and power tools, and at a central location for convenience.

All connections are marked on the floorplan. In the figure, the labeling scheme follows the office numbers.

When a network is installed in an existing structure, the cable is generally run through the ceiling and dropped down the walls to a connector installed in the wall. In a bus or ring network, the wall connector represents the connection point to the network. The same convention is followed in the figure. Where possible, the cable is run so that it lies perpendicular to the fluorescent lights. In those parts of the building where that isn't possible, the cable runs a minimum of twelve inches from the lights.

Avoiding sources of interference requires more cable and is a consequent cost factor. However, it is wiser to spend money on additional cable than to tear the cable out later and reinstall it.

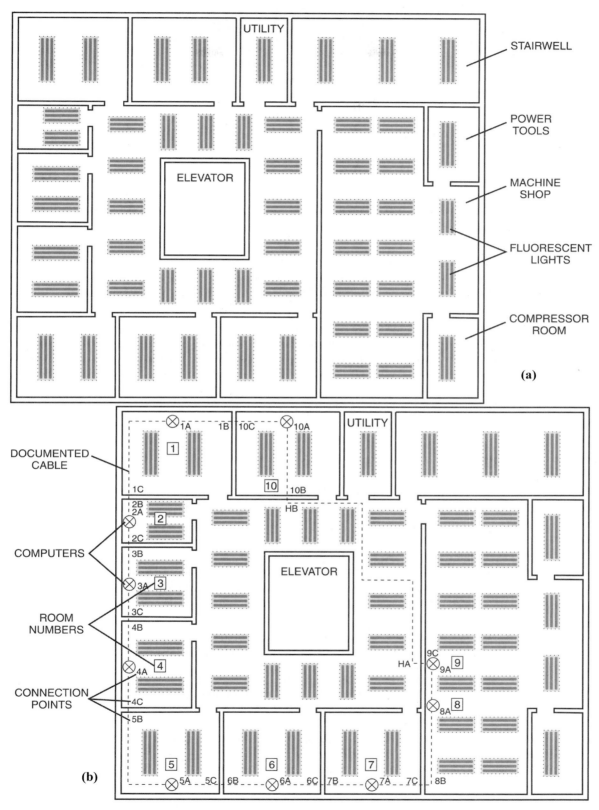

Figure 2-1: Developing a Network Floorplan

GUIDELINES FOR CABLING INSTALLATION

- Pinpoint the location of each PC in an office.

- Use wiring that meets the specifications of the network.

- Avoid mixing cable types, either by brand names or by part numbers. If a different cable must be used, a repeater is recommended at the cable junction.

- Consult building codes to determine if your network cable meets the local requirements. Some codes require that twisted pair be run through the conduit. However, this may cause the data signal to be attenuated. In a case such as this, either use another cable type, or install repeaters to boost the signal strength.

- When using twisted pairs, maintain wiring polarity throughout the network. For CAT5 UTP, this means ensuring that the wire pairs are not crossed-over for a hub connection.

- Avoid electromagnetic radiation by maintaining a distance of 12 inches from fluorescent lighting, 40 inches from transformers and motors, 6 inches from power lines carrying 2 kVA or less, 12 inches from power lines carrying 2 to 5 kVA, and at least 36 inches from power lines carrying more than 5 kVA.

- Cross 120Vac lines at right angles.

- Anticipate the movement of PCs in an office. In an Ethernet network, the maximum cable distance run from the PC to the tap connection is 8 feet. Install the tap boxes to accommodate the rearrangement of offices.

- Check to ensure that all mechanical connections are tight.

- Label wall jack connections with a permanent marker. If wall jacks are not used, ensure that the color code continuity of the cable is kept consistent throughout the network. As an alternative to color coding, label each cable end with wire tape.

- On the floorplan, document the corresponding connections of the wire labels. This is particularly important if the wires are concealed behind walls or in the ceiling. Many networks feed to a central hub or wiring harness. The labeled wire feeding the harness should have a corresponding label at the opposite end of the cable, and the labeling annotations should be documented on the floorplan.

Figure 2-2: Cabling Installation Guidelines

CABLE TYPES AND TYPICAL APPLICATIONS			
Cable type	**Typical applications**	**Speed (Mbps)**	**Distance limitation**
Coaxial Cable			
Thick 50 ohm (yellow)	IEEE 802.3 10Base5 Ethernet LAN	10	500 meters per segment
Thin 50 ohm (RG-58)	IEEE 802.3 10Base2 Cheapernet LAN	10	185 meters per segment
Broadband 75 ohm (RG-6 or RG-11)	IEEE 802.3 10Broad36 Ethernet LAN	5 and 10	3600 meters between nodes
	IEEE 802.4 Token Bus LAN (factory)	5 and 10	3600 meters between nodes
	Various combinations of video, voice, and data	1 to 5 per 6 MHz channel (400 MHz BW)	3600 meters between nodes
Coax 93 ohm (RG-62)	Systems Network Architecture (SNA) network (IBM 3270)	1	1640 meters
Twinax 100 ohm	SNA network (IBM System 3/X-AS/400)	1	1640 meters
Fiber-Optic Cable			
Single-mode fiber	FDDI LAN	100	40 km link lengths
	Long-haul, high-speed video, voice, and data	Limited by active components	Hundreds of Mb miles
Multimode fiber	IEEE 802.3 10BaseF Ethernet LAN	10	500-2000 m (node type)
	ISDN DS0 (1 voice) DS1 (24 voice) (without compression)	64 kbps 1.544	Depends on node type and components used
	FDDI LAN	100	2 km between nodes 100 km total circumference
	IEEE 802.4 Token Bus LAN (factory)	5 and 10	Node type and components
	IEEE 802.5 Token Ring LAN	4 and 16	Node type and components
	Various combinations of voice and data	300 Mb/miles/sec	500-2000 meters depending on node type
Unshielded Twisted Pair Cable			
IBM Type 3 (and regular telephone service)	IEEE 802.5 Token Ring LAN	1	100 meters
CAT3 or CAT5	IEEE 802.3 10BaseT Ethernet LAN	10	100 meters
CAT5	IEEE 802.3 100Base-Tx	100	100 meters
RS-232	Serial communications	19.2 kbps	15-30 meters
RS-442 ISDN	EIA RS-442 DS0 (1 voice)	1 64 kbps x 2	1300 meters 1950 meters
T-1	DS1 (24 voice)	1.544	1950 meters

Figure 2-3: Cable Characteristics

There are many different cabling schemes. Figures 2-4, 2-5, and 2-6 show several examples of common arrangements.

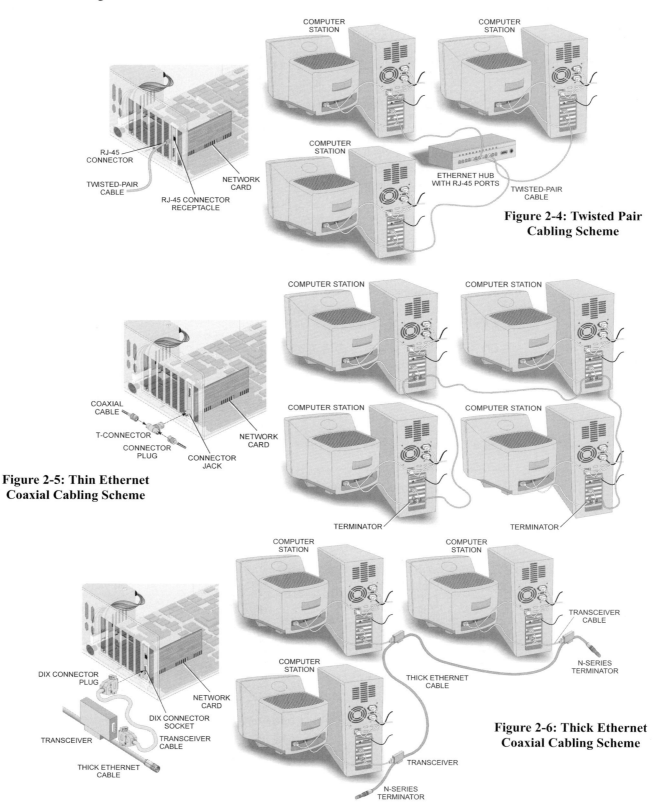

Figure 2-4: Twisted Pair Cabling Scheme

Figure 2-5: Thin Ethernet Coaxial Cabling Scheme

Figure 2-6: Thick Ethernet Coaxial Cabling Scheme

Figure 2-7 illustrates the floorplan of a single-floor, industrial control research facility. The rooms to the left of the diagram are offices. The rectangles represent overhead fluorescent lighting. In the right top corner is a laboratory equipped with high-voltage instruments arranged in a bank on the outside wall. The section marked "work room" contains two areas equipped with various types of industrial controls. Assume that the controls operate from a wide range of voltages and include motors, pneumatics, and hydraulics.

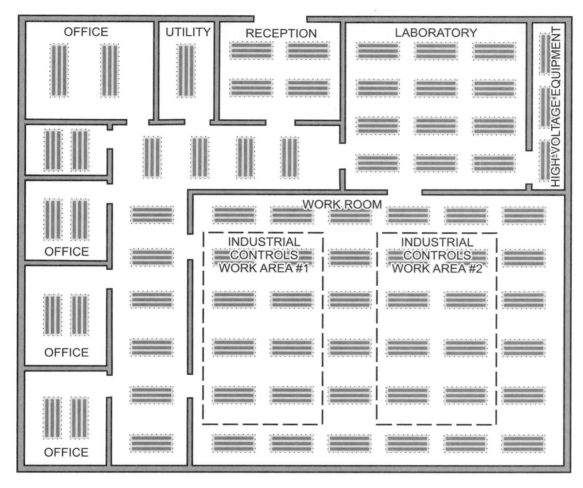

Figure 2-7: Floorplan Exercise

1. On Figure 2-7, you are to sketch a bus style network in a manner similar to that of Figure 2-1(b). The reception area, and each office, is to contain a single PC. The lab is to be equipped with two PCs and the workroom will contain six PCs. This represents a total of 14 computers.

2. Position the computers in each room and select a network cable type. Then, sketch the cable run through the building.

3. Devise a system for labeling all connections, and write the label designations on the connections.

4. Once you've determined a cabling system that appears to address the common electrical interference problems, write two standard operating procedures.

   • The first will be titled Cable Installation.
   • The second will be called Cable Labeling Scheme.

PROCEDURE - 2

Use the basic format shown in Figure 2-8 as a template for creating the procedure. At a minimum, your SOPs must contain a Title, Date, Revision Code, and Approval List in the heading. The body of the SOP must include Purpose and Procedure fields. If you use Microsoft Word or Corel WordPerfect, try linking the two documents to an Index that contains these two titles. This way, you'll create a paperless controlled documentation system.

STANDARD OPERATING PROCEDURE	
TITLE:	
REVISION:	DATE:
APPROVALS:	
REVISION HISTORY:	
DISTRIBUTION LIST:	
SCOPE AND OBJECTIVE	
PROCEDURE	
RELEVANT PROCEDURES, FORMS, AND MANUALS	

Figure 2-8: SOP Template

Feedback

LAB QUESTIONS

1. Of the three basic network topologies—bus, ring, and star—would you recommend a topology other than bus for the floorplan of Figure 2-7? Why?
2. What type of cable media did you select? Why?
3. Assume that, in the future, a second building is needed and it's constructed a mile away. How will the computers in the two buildings communicate? Draw a square at the bottom of Figure 2-7 representing the new building. Illustrate the components needed to network the computers in the two buildings.
4. Without the benefit of a detailed floorplan showing the connecting points in a bus network, how would you determine the connections needed to create a plan? In a ring network? A star network?
5. Describe the potential effect of working on a cabling problem with unlabeled cable connections.
6. If another computer is added to the network used in the Lab, why should the floorplan be updated?

Assembling and Testing Network Cables

OBJECTIVES

1. Identify an RJ-45 connector.
2. Identify the wire pairs of a CAT5 UTP cable according to the specification in EIA/TIA 568A.
3. Prepare a CAT5 cable for an RJ-45 connector.
4. Using a commercial crimping tool, add RJ-45 connectors to both ends of a CAT5 cable.
5. Using a D200 Cable Tester, check the cable for opens and shorts, reversed wire pairs, and correct connections.

Hardware Exploration

RESOURCES

1. Network+ Certification Training Guide
2. A length of CAT5 UTP cable
3. Two RJ-45 connectors
4. Exacto knife or wire strippers
5. RJ-45 crimping tool

DISCUSSION

Networks may be wired with one of three types of cabling: twisted pairs, coaxial cable, and fiber optic. Currently, twisted pairs are the most widely installed cabling medium in the industry. The most important reason for its popularity is it's the lowest-priced medium on a cost-per-foot basis. The next—and some may argue the most important reason—is its high data rate capabilities. The data rates of certain types of twisted pair cabling far exceed those of coaxial cable in a baseband network; that is, a network that doesn't use a carrier separate from the data that's transmitted.

Since twisted pairs are so widely used, this Lab Procedure focuses on them, but also includes step-by-step procedures for adding connectors to coaxial cables. Once end connectors are added to a twisted pair cable, it must be tested to ensure continuity and the correct connections between each end. So, once you assemble connectors to a twisted pair cable, you'll use a commercial cable tester to make sure it's wired together properly. This is critical in a network because most installation problems can be traced to cable errors.

Twisted pairs are classified by Category. Figure 3-1 describes the category types and includes data rate specifications for each type. For this Lab, and all other Lab Procedures in this course, you'll use only category 5 (CAT5) unshielded twisted pair (UTP) cables. CAT5 UTP has become the industry standard for UTP cabling and should be used in all new installations.

CAT5 UTP supports data rates in excess of 100 Mbps. This is far higher than baseband networks using co-axial cable but much less than networks that use fiber optic. While fiber optic is capable of achieving higher data rates, it's also more expensive and more difficult to install. It also lends itself to certain types of installations more readily than other types.

EIA/TIA UNSHIELDED TWISTED PAIR SPECIFICATION

Category 1—This is 22 or 24 AWG untwisted wire, known as common telephone cable. This is the cable that is used to connect many telephones to phone drops, and to connect extensions within a building.

Category 2—This is 22 or 24 AWG solid wire, in twisted pairs. CAT2 was the first networking UTP, but is now considered obsolete. It supports data rates up to 1 Mbps and is not tested for crosstalk distortion.

Category 3—This is 24 AWG solid wire, in twisted pairs. Originally used in IBM Token Ring LANs, CAT3 is seldom used outside an IBM environment, and has been replaced by CAT4 cabling. CAT3 is occasionally used in 10 Mbps Ethernet LANs as well as 4 Mbps Token Ring LANs. It has been tested for data rates up to 16 Mbps. The wire has a characteristic impedance of 100 ohms.

Category 4—This is 22 or 24 AWG solid wire, in twisted pairs. This category has been specified for up to 20 Mbps and is specified for 16 Mbps Token Ring LANs. The wire has a characteristic impedance of 100 ohms.

Category 5—This is 22 or 24 AWG solid wire, in twisted pairs. CAT5 cable has a characteristic impedance of 100 ohms and is specified for data rates up to 100 Mbps. This is the preferred cabling installation for Ethernet and Token Ring, and is recommended for all new installations, even if an existing LAN is running at 10 Mbps (standard Ethernet speeds). If you choose to upgrade to the 100 Mbps Fast Ethernet, the cabling will already be installed and ready to go.

Figure 3-1: UTP Categories

CAT5 cable consists of eight solid wires, which may range in diameter from about 22 to 26 AWG (American Wire Gauge). The eight wires are enclosed in an outer jacket. To be used in a network, the cable is fixed with an end connector. Almost universally, the end connector is an RJ-45 connector.

Figure 3-2 illustrates an RJ-45 connector. Its appearance is very similar to that of a normal telephone connector (which is an RJ-11) except that the RJ-45 is larger. Of the eight wires in a CAT5 cable, a local area network typically uses only four, and these are separated into two pairs. One pair is called the transmit pair, the other is called the receive pair.

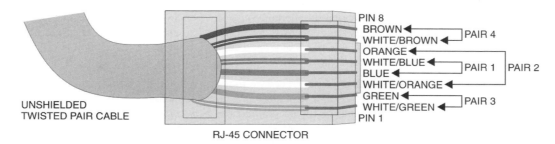

Figure 3-2: RJ-45 Connector

It's extremely important to designate which wire pairs will be used for transmitting, and which will be used for receiving. Figure 3-3 shows the EIA/TIA specification for establishing the pairing of wires in a CAT5 UTP. You must decide whether to follow EIA/TIA 568A or 568B in an installation. Once the decision is made, you must remain consistent for all UTP cable. If not, you'll create situations where one node is trying to transmit on a wire pair that another node is sending on.

WIRE COLOR	EIA/TIA PAIR	ETHERNET SIGNAL USE	
		568A	568B
White/Blue (W-BL)	Pair 1	Not Used	
Blue (BL)			
White/Orange (W-OR)	Pair 2	RX+	TX+
Orange (OR)		RX–	TX–
White/Green (W-GR)	Pair 3	TX+	RX+
Green (GR)		TX–	RX–
White/Brown (W-BR)	Pair 4	Not Used	
Brown (BR)			

Figure 3-3: EIA/TIA 586 Standard

For this course, you'll use EIA/TIA 568A. This is the standard you should follow for all UTP cables in this course. Wire pair two will be the receive pair, and wire pair three will be the transmit pair.

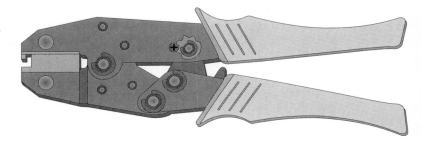

Now that we have an agreed-upon standard process for adding connectors to CAT5 UTP, let's get started. You'll use a commercial crimping tool, as shown in Figure 3-4, to attach the RJ-45 connector to each pair. But first, the wires need to be prepared.

Figure 3-4: Crimping Tool

Hardware Exploration

PROCEDURE

1. Start with a length of CAT5 UTP cable. See your instructor for the appropriate length.

2. Using an Exacto knife or pair of wire strippers, remove about 3 inches of the outer insulating jacket at each end of the cable.

3. Separate each pair of wires and put them in the correct order of sequence according to the EIA/TIA specification for 568A, as shown in Figure 3-2.

4. Snip the wires to about 1 inch from the outer insulating jacket.

5. With the hook side of the RJ-45 connector facing down, slide the wires all the way into the connector. Push the outer insulating jacket into the connector just past the first crimping point.

6. Place the RJ-45 connector into the crimping tool. Firmly pull the handle of the tool until the wires are crimped into place.

7. Each of the wires should be crimped tightly by the connector, and the outer jacket should be bound by the connector. If any of the wires can be pulled from the connector with a gentle tug, the connection is incorrect. If the edge of the outer jacket isn't sealed in the crimp, the connection is also incorrect.

8. To make a complete cable, repeat the steps above and add a connector to the other end of the cable.

A common and easy to use cable tester is the D200 LAN Cable Tester, shown in Figure 3-5. This model is used to detect lack of continuity between any of the wires, to check if the wires are paired properly, and to see if any of the wire pairs are crossed.

Figure 3-5: D200 LAN Cable Tester

To use the tester, connect one RJ-45 connector to one of the units, and the other to the other unit. You'll receive one of the following results:

- If all LEDs illuminate green, the cable checks good.
- If red LEDs are illuminated, the wire pairs are reversed.
- If an LED isn't illuminated, there's an open between the wires of one or both pairs.

Note that it's important to wire the connectors according the EIA/TIA standard in order for this cable tester to check the wire.

The advantage of a cable tester such as the D200 LAN Cable Tester is that you can connect one module to one end of a cable that's located in a remote room such as a hub and wiring closet. The other end can be connected at the opposite end of the cable, which may be at the client computer. In other words, it allows you to be in two places at once.

9. Check the CAT5 cable you constructed with RJ-45 connectors by plugging one end of the cable to the 10BaseT connector of the Remote module. Plug the other end of the cable into the 10BaseT connector of the Master module. Record the results of your test in Table 3-1.

Coaxial cables were the first cable type used in LANs. It's called "coaxial" because the center conductor and outer shield share the same axis. Figure 3-6 shows the structure of a coaxial cable. It consists of the following:

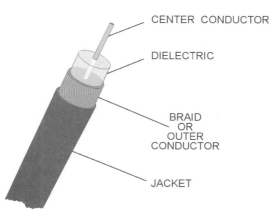

CENTER CONDUCTOR

DIELECTRIC

BRAID
OR
OUTER
CONDUCTOR

JACKET

- **Center Conductor:** A solid copper wire. Occasionally, the center conductor is made of stranded wire.
- **Outer Conductor:** Encircles the center conductor. The outer conductor may be made from braided wires, metallic foil, or both. Frequently called the shield, it serves as a ground and also protects the inner conductor from EMI (electromagnetic interference).
- **Dielectric:** An insulation layer that keeps the outer conductor spaced evenly from the inner conductor.
- **Jacket:** Protects the cable from damage.

Coaxial cable used in networking installation may be classified as thicknet or thinnet.

Thinnet, used in 10Base2 installations, is lightweight and fairly easy to work with. It has a characteristic impedance of 50 ohms and is limited to a maximum length of 185 meters in a network.

Figure 3-6: Coaxial Cable

Thicknet, used in 10Base5 installations, is far more rigid and difficult to install. It also has a characteristic impedance of 50 ohms. Thicknet cable has a thicker center conductor than thinnet; this is why the maximum segment length of thicknet is greater than that of thinnet.

Note that the impedance of a cable isn't related to the length of the cable. Any length will exhibit 50 ohms OS resistance to a data signal. When connected in a bus topology, both types of coaxial cable must be terminated at the ends of the bus with a 50-ohm resistance in order to prevent signal reflections. Thicknet can transmit a signal approximately 500 meters (1,650 feet).

Perform the following steps for adding end connectors to a coaxial cable:

10. Begin with a length of thinnet coaxial cable.

11. Locate two twist-on BNC (British Naval Connector) connectors, and set them aside.

12. Strip back three-quarters of an inch of the outer insulation, being careful not to cut the center conductor or shielding

13. Strip about one-half inch of the shielding and plastic insulator from around the center conductor.

This will leave approximately one-quarter of an inch of exposed shielding.

14. Peel the shielding away from the center plastic insulator so that one-eighth of an inch of the insulator is exposed.

15. Twist the outer-braid in a clockwise direction so that the shielding is left flat.

16. Gently insert the center conductor into the back end of the connector.

You'll feel the plastic insulator slip into the guide-hole. The cable is in place when the back of the connector is flush with the exposed shielding of the cable.

17. Push the cable firmly until you meet resistance.

18. Screw the connector onto the cable in a clockwise direction.

19. Repeat the same steps described above for the other end of the cable.

TABLES

Table 3-1: EIA/TIA 586 Standard

CAT5 RJ-45 CABLE TEST RESULTS		
Wire Pair	**LED Indication**	**Result (Good/Bad)**
Wire Pair 1 and 2		
Wire Pair 3 and 6		
Wire Pair 4 and 5		
Wire Pair 7 and 8		

Feedback

LAB QUESTIONS

1. What category of UTP is recommended for new network installations?
2. What type of connector is used with CAT5 cable?
3. Which wire pairs are used for transmit in a CAT5 cable? Which wire pairs are used for receiving in a CAT5 cable?
4. The LEDs on a D200 LAN Cable Tester show dark at pairs 4-5 and 7-8. What does this mean?
5. Refer to Question 4. Can this cable be used in a 10BaseT network? Explain your answer.

Installing and Testing a Modem

OBJECTIVES

1. Install an internal modem into an available expansion slot of a personal computer.
2. Configure the modem using the Windows Plug-and-Play installation process.
3. Describe how to configure a modem that isn't Plug-and-Play, or fully software-configurable.
4. Check the modem using diagnostics software.
5. Document the essential parameters of a modem to establish a baseline reference before and after making changes.

RESOURCES

1. Network+ Certification Training Guide
2. Windows 2000 Professional workstation
3. An analog modem
4. The modem vendor's specification and installation instructions

Hardware Exploration

Software Exploration

DISCUSSION

Modem is an acronym for modulator/demodulator. Typically, when you speak of a modem, you're talking about a circuit card that's placed in an expansion slot of a computer and is used to format data so it can be sent and received across the analog portion of the telephone system. In other words, "modem" normally refers to an analog modem.

There are, however, other types of modems. A cable modem, for example, is used to format data so it can be sent and received across the coaxial or fiber cable that's used for cable television access. A so-called digital modem is used for connection to the digital side of the telephone system although it's not technically a modem. ISDN, for example, requires that an ISDN adapter be installed at the subscriber site, and these are sometimes incorrectly called modems. A T-Carrier connection also requires specialized equipment at the subscriber site but, again, the device isn't a modem although you may hear it referred to as a digital modem.

Analog modems are described in terms of how fast they operate. The current speed for them is a maximum of 56 kbps, although this data rate can't be achieved in actual practice. The fastest analog modems are those that operate across the analog portion of the local telephone loop—about 48 kbps. These modems are specified in the ITU standard V.90.

Not all modems are installed in an expansion slot of a PC. Some modems are external, meaning they're stand-alone devices that connect to the telephone system with one jack (an RJ-11 connector) and to a port on a computer with another jack (either serial or parallel). Neither has an advantage over the other although internal modems may be a bit cheaper since they don't need a case, chassis, etc. Figure 4-1 shows an example of an internal and an external modem.

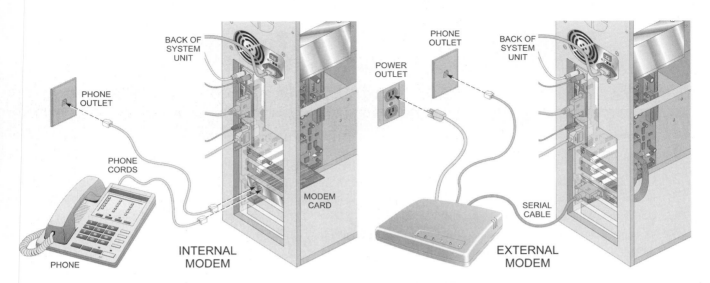

Figure 4-1: Internal and External Modems

One thing to keep in mind is that a modem is specialized. An analog modem isn't compatible with an ISDN adapter even though both connect to the telephone network via RJ-11 jacks.

In this Lab Procedure, you'll install and test an analog modem using Windows Plug-and-Play installation software. A PnP device is fully software/configurable. Older modems contain switches that are used to change the configuration of the modem, and many of these modems are still in use, so we'll take a brief look at an example of how to configure a modem with DIP switches as well.

PROCEDURE

Hardware Exploration

Follow these steps to install a modem into an expansion slot of a PC.

1. Turn off power to the PC and remove its cover.

2. Locate an available expansion slot.

Figure 4-2 shows a typical PCI expansion slot used for installing a modem.

3. Select a slot that will allow you easy access to the back of the card. You may need to periodically insert and remove the telephone connections.

4. Ground yourself to prevent electrostatic damage by slipping on an antistatic wrist strap. Then remove the modem from its antistatic bag.

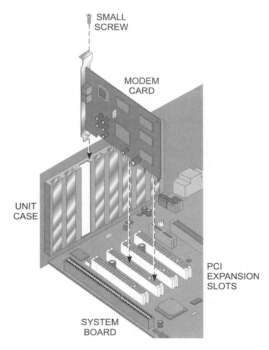

Figure 4-2: Identifying PC Expansion Slots

5. Install the card into the expansion slot. Make sure the card is evenly seated. Secure it tightly to the system's rear chassis using an installation screw.

6. Replace the cover and turn on the power to the unit.

Notice that the modem doesn't need to be connected to the telephone to be configured. When the power is applied, PnP should locate the new hardware and prompt to install the modem.

7. Follow the prompts to install the modem. If Plug and Play doesn't detect the modem, follow the next steps. If it does, skip to step 15.

8. Navigate the *Start/Setting/Control Panel* path and click on the **Phone and Modem Options** icon.

Software Exploration

Windows may not find the new hardware, and if it doesn't, continue with the following steps to go to the installation screen.

9. Click on the **Modems** tab and choose **Add**. A window similar to Figure 4-3 will appear.

Note that the window has a field that prompts to detect the new modem. It is generally a good idea to let Windows detect new hardware or software, unless you have a good reason not to do so.

10. Click on the **Next** button.

Once the modem is found, or not found, which is a possibility, you'll be prompted to finish the install. Figure 4-4 shows a screen in which you select a modem from a list of modems for which Windows has preinstalled drivers.

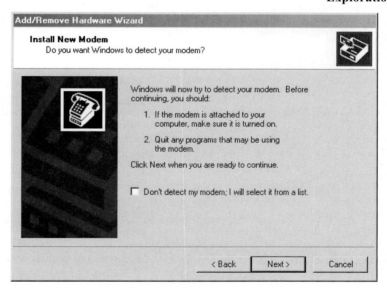

Figure 4-3: Install New Modem

If your modem is relatively new compared to the date that you purchased the Windows software, choose Have Disk. The drivers included with the modem may be newer than those bundled with your version of Windows.

11. Click on the **Have Disk** button.

You will be taken to a dialog box that allows you to install the drivers from a floppy drive, or a CD-ROM disc.

Figure 4-4: Modem Type Selection

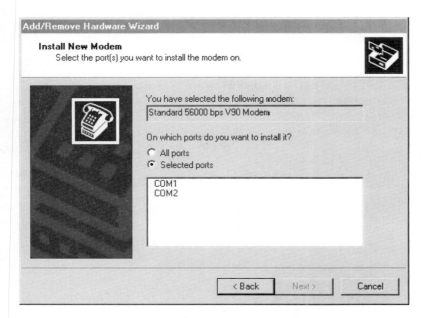

Figure 4-5: Modem COM Port Selection

12. Install the driver for your specific modem.

If you need help, ask your instructor. Once the drivers are installed, the screen shown in Figure 4-5 will open.

13. Now you must select a COM port for the modem. Choose **COM 2**. This will default to Interrupt ReQuest (IRQ) 3.

The software will complete the process and you'll be finished with the installation and configuration.

14. Click on the **Finish** button at the end of the installation.

Now you need to test the modem. The quickest way to do this is to communicate with another modem, but the most common method is to connect to the Internet. However, if you're not hooked up you can use Windows' diagnostics by doing the following:

15. From the Control Panel, click on the **Phone and Modem Options** icon.

For initial installations, a dialog box requesting country and area codes will appear.

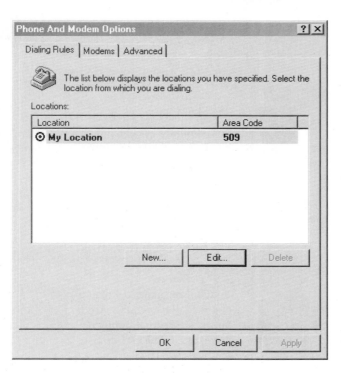

Figure 4-6: Modem Properties

16. If you are asked for the country and area codes, enter them and click on the **Close** button.

The *Phone And Modem Options* window, similar to that shown in Figure 4-6, will open.

17. Click on the **Modems** tab.

18. Highlight your modem and click on Properties.

19. Click on the **Diagnostics** tab.

20. Click on the **Query Modem** button.

You'll receive a message telling you that Windows is communicating with the modem. Momentarily the results of the diagnostic test will be shown in the dialog box. The box will display information about your modem, as shown in Figure 4-7.

Of particular interest are the commands listed at the bottom of the box. These are Hayes AT commands for your modem. The AT commands control the functionality of modems. Notice that next to each command is an assortment of information that was generated. This means that the modem passed the diagnostic test because the computer software can communicate with the modem hardware.

Windows diagnostics for modems isn't a full test because it doesn't test the ability of the modem to send and receive files to a distant modem. But it sometimes detects discrepancies such as port and IRQ conflicts, as well as faulty seating of the modem card.

If the computer restarts and no problems are detected in the diagnostics test, your modem will probably work. In a later Lab Procedure, you'll check to see how well it actually works.

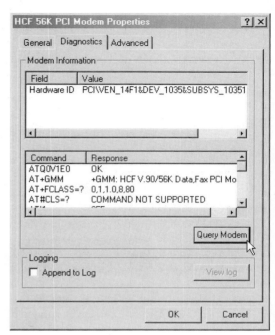

Figure 4-7: Modem Diagnostics

Recall that some modems aren't PnP capable because the configuration for these types of modems is accomplished with a combination of hardware settings and software installation. Figure 4-8 shows the DIP switch settings for an older modem. Next to the DIP switch is a key illustrating the switch positions for one of four COM ports.

Figure 4-8: Hardware COM Port Settings

Even if you're replacing an older internal modem, it's important to note the positions of the DIP switches. These switches can indicate the configuration parameters that have been set up for the computer. If the new modem you're installing doesn't work for some reason, you may need to reinstall the original modem until you can figure out the problem. Table 4-1 is a simple chart that can be used to document the parameters for any modem you install. Take a few minutes and complete the information for the install you just completed. If you don't know the values, perform the following steps to determine them.

21. Right-click on the **My Computer** icon and choose the **Properties** option.

22. Click on the **Hardware** tab and click on the **Device Manager** button.

23. Expand the *Modems* icon and the modem you've installed will appear beneath the *Modem* icon. Double-click on your modem.

24. A *Modem Properties* window, shown in Figure 4-9, will open.

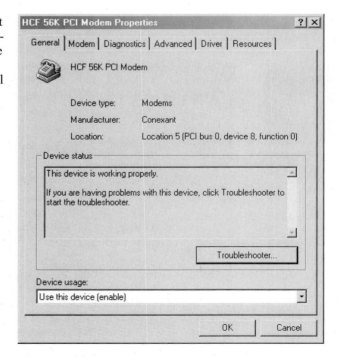

Figure 4-9: Modem Properties

25. To check the COM port, click on the **Modem** tab.

26. To check the base I/O address and IRQ settings, click on the **Resources** tab.

27. To check the connection parameters, click on the **Advanced** tab, click on **Change Default preferences**, and choose the **Advanced** tab.

28. Complete the values indicated in Table 4-1.

TABLES

Table 4-1: Modem Card Parameters

MODEM CONFIGURATION	
COM Port	
Base I/O Range	
IRQ	
Data Bits	
Parity	
Stop Bits	

Feedback

LAB QUESTIONS

1. How is a Plug-and-Play modem configured?

2. A 28.8 kbps modem is being replaced with a V.90 modem. Before making the change, how will you document the current configuration of the 28.8 kbps modem?

3. Describe how to run diagnostics on a newly installed modem.

Using Modem Commands

OBJECTIVES

1. View the configuration settings of a modem.
2. Set up the Windows HyperTerminal program.
3. Check communication between the computer and the modem using Hayes AT commands.

Software Exploration

RESOURCES

1. Network+ Certification Training Guide
2. Windows 2000 Professional workstation with an analog modem installed
3. Hayes AT commands for the installed modem

DISCUSSION

The functionality of a modem is contained in the Hayes AT Command Set. These are software commands used to configure the modem. In Windows-based software, much of the configuration is implemented within dialog boxes. AT commands can tell you quite a bit about your modem. Unfortunately, not all modem manufacturers give you easy access to them, and those who do don't always make it easy. It takes a little experimenting. Be cautious when nosing around in the AT commands because if you make a change, this changes how your modem works.

Table 4-4, in the textbook, shows a partial list of AT commands. While these are typical, they may differ from those on your modem because each manufacturer implements the commands a little differently. The next section explains how to view the command set.

Currently, three vendors manufacture 56k modem chips—Rockwell, Lucent Technologies, and 3Com/U. S. Robotics. All of them use Hayes AT commands and all three implement them differently. Before using them, you need to know the chip manufacturer of your modem. Read the modem documentation or look at the modem card to see who made the chip. A couple of hundred commands are used to configure a modem if it includes data/fax/voice capabilities. Most of these you'll never need, but some are very useful in learning about your modem and troubleshooting it.

Software Exploration

PROCEDURE

1. Navigate the *Start/Settings/Control Panel* path and click on the **Phone and Modem Options** icon.

2. Click on the **Modems** tab.

3. Select your modem by highlighting it and click on the **Properties** button.

Another dialog box opens, which contains configuration data about your modem, such as the COM port it is using, its speaker volume, the word length of data it will process, its maximum operating speed, number of stop bits it is using, and so on. These are the same parameters you recorded in the previous Lab Procedure. The information you see in these boxes is normally contained in the NVRAM (Non-Volatile Random Access Memory) chip on the modem card. AT commands allow you to access the NVRAM to see what you're currently using. A modem that uses the Hayes AT Command Set is said to be Hayes Compatible.

You can learn quite a bit about your modem from AT commands. To do so, you first need to set up the HyperTerminal program in Windows 9x/NT (or Terminal in Windows 3.x).

4. HyperTerminal is installed in Windows 2000 by default. You can run the program by navigating the *Start/Programs/Accessories/HyperTerminal* path.

The *Connection Description* window, shown in Figure 5-1, appears.

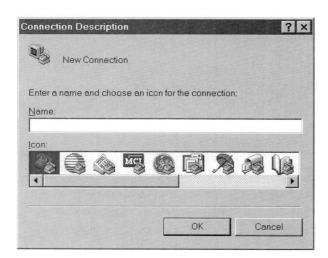

Figure 5-1: Connection Description Box

6. Enter **555-5555** for a telephone number. You won't be dialing out.

7. Click on the **OK** button.

Once the numbering information is entered, Windows will ask you if you want to connect.

5. Enter a name for the terminal session such as Test Terminal, and click on **OK**.

The *Connect To* window will now appear, as shown in Figure 5-2. As you can see, it contains telephone number information.

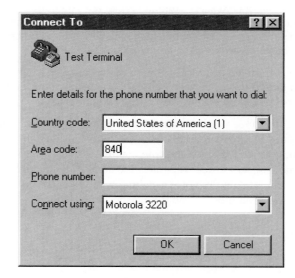

Figure 5-2: Connect To Dialog Box

8. Click on the **Cancel** button, and a blank HyperTerminal screen will appear on your monitor, as shown in Figure 5-3.

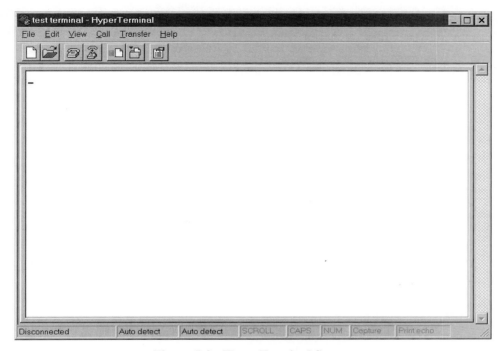

Figure 5-3: HyperTerminal Screen

9. Type **AT** and press ENTER.

The screen should respond with OK. This is a quick test that checks to see whether the computer can communicate with the modem. If you get an OK, it means that the communication software is able to communicate with the modem hardware.

10. If you weren't able to see the letters when typing the command AT, try typing **ATE1** and pressing the ENTER key.

If the letters you type now appear on the screen, it means that the echo command was previously turned off, making it impossible to see your own typing. Keep in mind that pressing the ENTER key after typing each command is always necessary in order to execute it.

If, after entering AT, the screen responds with ERROR, the program is telling you that the test failed. Or, in other words, HyperTerminal can't find your modem. Either the COM port you've selected for the modem is incorrect, or some other device is currently using it.

11. Figure 5-4 lists several basic commands for each of the three modem chip vendors. Determine which modem you're using, and try them out.

Keep in mind that some commands will produce varied results depending on the chip manufacturer. For a complete listing of all AT commands, go to the web site of each vendor and download data sheets for their respective chips.

Figure 5-4: Hayes AT Commands

ROCKWELL	
COMMAND	**DESCRIPTION**
AT	Switch from data mode to command mode.
AT/	Re-execute the last command.
ATEI	Turn on the command echo.
ATI0	Report the product code.
ATI1	Compute and report the checksum.
ATIX2	Report basic call progress codes and connection speeds.
AT&V	Display the current configuration.
AT$V1	Display the statistics on the last connection.
3COM/U.S. ROBOTICS	
COMMAND	**DESCRIPTION**
AT	Switch from data mode to command mode.
ATI2	Perform a RAM test.
ATI4	Show the current settings.
ATI5	Show the NVRAM settings.
ATI6	Display the statistics on the last connection.
ATI7	Display the product configuration.
AT$	Display the Help list of AT commands.
LUCENT TECHNOLOGIES	
COMMAND	**DESCRIPTION**
AT	Switch from data mode to command mode.
ATI3	Show the firmware version.
ATI11	Display the statistics on the last connection.

12. Use the chart shown in Figure 5-4 to record the AT commands you entered in Table 5-1, along with a description of the results.

TABLES

Table 5-1: AT Commands and Results

AT COMMANDS AND RESULTS	
AT COMMAND	**RESULT**

LAB QUESTIONS

Feedback

1. Describe how to view the configuration settings for an installed modem.
2. You enter the Hayes command AT and see nothing on the screen. What does this mean?
3. You enter AT and the screen responds with OK. What does this mean?

Measuring Modem Speeds

**Software
Exploration**

OBJECTIVES

1. Create a system for establishing a base reference to measure modem transfer rates.
2. Use appropriate Hayes AT commands to access data transfer rates.
3. Compare the transfer rates of two different client computers.

RESOURCES

1. Network+ Certification Training Guide
2. Two Windows 2000 Professional workstations with installed modems
3. Phone Simulation hardware
4. Hayes AT commands for the installed modem
5. HyperTerminal software
6. 1MB test image from the Network+ CD
7. Vendor documentation for modem

DISCUSSION

A V.90 modem sends data at one rate and receives it at another. The receive rate is much faster than the send rate. A 33.6 kbps modem, on the other hand, sends and receives at about the same rate. In some cases, neither modem will connect at its specified rate, but at some lower one.

The capabilities of the distant server affect how fast data will be transferred to a local machine. On a worldwide network, a wide range of download rates are simultaneously occurring on it at any given second. A modem has fallback rates that are intended to match the speed capabilities of a distant modem so that if it's an older and slower device, the connection will fall back to whatever rate it can reliably send and receive.

Also affecting data rates are the CPU speed of the local machine, the size and type of the data bus in the machine, and the buffering used to cache the received data. A PC routinely caches data, but a modem has its own cache—or buffer, as it's called. If the modem's buffer is full (which occurs at about 70% of its maximum size), the data will be off-loaded to the system cache, or RAM. If any of these factors are limited, a download will appear to be slow, even if it's transferring at the maximum speed. If any of these factors are limited, a download will appear to be slow, even if it's transferring at the maximum speed across the line connection. What's needed is an objective approach to establishing a baseline reference for measuring the speed of data transfers. A user may complain that his/her connection is slow, and what you will have to determine is the reason for it. Is it the modem? Is it a lack of RAM in the client? Does the client CPU need to be upgraded to a Pentium III microprocessor? Should the amount of reserved cache be increased?

The following Lab can be used to provide a reference for measuring the speed of a data transfer. What you should be able to determine is the bit speed of a transfer, along with the time it takes to download a sizable file from a remote server. Based upon the data presented, you'll be able to decide if the modem is working at peak efficiency.

Software Exploration

PROCEDURE

One of the most accurate ways to check transfers between your modem and a known distant server is to up-load and/or download a file between the local machine (client) and the server of an Internet Service Pro-vider (ISP). However, in networks where no Internet connection is provided, alternate techniques can be employed to measure the speed of modem file transfers.

For example, a hardware phone simulator can be used to act as a type of telephone switchboard to provide the switching circuitry and subscriber line voltages normally supplied by the public telephone company. It can be designed to accept any combination of digital dialing tones as a legitimate sequence for the purpose of completing a call between two modems (or telephones). Most phone simulators can also operate in an al-ternate mode capable of signaling the remote modem (or telephone) automatically, as soon as the local unit goes off-hook.

At this point, you have installed a modem into a computer and you have already tested the ability of the modem and the computer to communicate with each other. What you now want to determine is the ability of your computer to communicate with a remote computer that is also outfitted with a modem. Once that communication is established, you'll want to download/upload a file that is large enough to reach an in-formed conclusion as to the modem's speed capabilities. You'll need to record the data transfer rate of your modem in both the receiving and transmitting directions.

One of the tricks about transferring data is the idea of taking large files (test or graphics) and compressing them using a client program such as WinZip. Once the compressed file is stored at the remote server, it can be used over and over for file downloads. Compressing a file before it is electronically transferred allows it to be sent much more quickly than would be possible in an uncompressed format. For your transfers you'll want to use one of these fairly large files (approximately 1 MB), and a file (**1MB test image.gif**) has al-ready been prepared (compressed) for you for this purpose. Because modems routinely compress files, un-less they have been compressed already, selecting a compressed file for transfer will allow you to know exactly how many bits are being sent.

The 1 MB test image.gif file is located on the Net+ CD that belongs to your particular workgroup. The lab room may be divided into several workgroups, each including its own server and client computers. The internal modems of two clients (not the server) will be connected directly to a phone simulator using stan-dard RJ-11–equipped cables because the phone simulator is equipped with two RJ-11 jacks, as shown in Figure 6-1.

Keep in mind that only two of the client machines can be connected to the phone simulator at any one time. Because the average transfer time for a 1 MB file is approximately five minutes, there should be more than enough time for both client computers to run the required transfers.

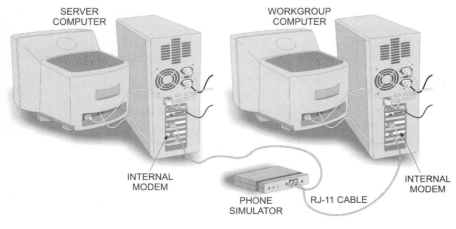

Figure 6-1: Server and Workgroup with Phone Simulator

For the purposes of the transfer, one client will assume the role of the serving computer.

In the real world (outside the classroom), downloading the same file at different times during the day and night would result in widely varying transfer rates because of the way in which network congestion affects them. Traffic would be heavier during the day and lightest in the middle of the night.

When recording your data transfer information, note whether your downloads are reported as bits or bytes. If bytes are reported, multiply the number of bytes by 9 to convert to bits. An error-correction protocol in the modem called V.42 removes stop/start bits during the conversion. However, because it adds some over-head of its own, 9 bits/byte remains a reasonable estimate. Once all of the testing has been completed, the transfer rates of the two clients can be compared in order to develop an average. If this average is used as a starting point for a base reference among the clients, any future deviations from the base reference may be used to indicate the need for network servicing.

You'll need a terminal program to run the communications session between the clients (one client acting as a server). Graphically based terminal programs aren't particularly accurate when reporting downloads since they're updating graphical changes. This makes it extremely difficult to extract actual data transfer rates using them. Windows comes with a fairly dependable communications application called HyperTerminal.

Because of several parameters that have been set up on the computer reserved for server duty during this course, this Lab Procedure will use two of the client machines, with one performing a so-called server function during the data transfer. Then the clients will switch their roles so that a file transfer can be accomplished in the opposite direction. With everything else being even, the two transfers should occur in about the same amount of time and at the same rate. Any large deviations in the results of these file transfers should be duly noted.

1. Decide which workstation will initially take the role of the serving computer. Copy the file named *1 MB test image.gif* to a temporary directory on the hard drive from the Network + CD.

2. Once the file is copied, make sure that both workstations (acting client and acting server) are shut down and turned off.

3. Connect an RJ-11–terminated telephone cable from one of the phone simulator's jacks to the phone in-put jack on the rear of the client computer's modem.

4. Connect a second RJ-11–terminated telephone cable from the remaining jack on the phone simulator to the phone input jack on the rear of the serving computer's modem.

5. Turn both the client and serving computers on, and allow the Windows desktop to appear on each.

6. Check to be sure that the phone simulator's Power/Mode switch is in the UP position, with the READY/ANSWER LED flashing green.

This places the phone simulator in its dialup mode.

7. From the Windows desktop on each machine, start the HyperTerminal program by navigating the *Start/Accessories/Communications* path, and then click on the **HyperTerminal** option.

8. On both computers, when the *Connection Description* box appears, enter a name for this terminal session, such as **Speed Test**, and click on **OK**.

9. At the *Connect To* dialog box, as shown in Figure 6-2, enter **555-5555** for a telephone number on both machines.

Figure 6-2: Entering Calling Number

PROCEDURE - 6

The phone simulator is designed to accept any legitimate series of numbers as a valid dialing sequence.

10. On both machines, click on the **OK** button.

Once the numbering information is entered, Windows will ask you if you want to connect.

11. On the serving machine, click on the **Cancel** button. Then, click through to the *Call/Wait for a call* option.

12. On the client machine, click on the **OK** button.

The HyperTerminal program will initiate a call from the client computer to the server and indicate on the screen when the connection is obtained, as well as the operating parameters under which the session will be conducted.

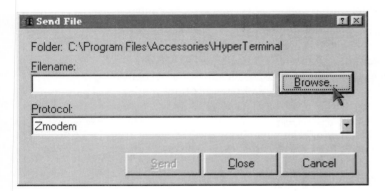

Figure 6-3: Browsing for a File to Send

13. Once the connection has been established, from the serving computer, click through to the *Transfer/Send File* option.

14. Observing Figure 6-3 on the serving computer, click on the **Browse** button.

15. Locate the test image file on the server and click on **Open**.

16. Click on the **Send** button.

As the file is transferred from the server to the client, HyperTerminal displays the progress of the operation on both machines, as shown in Figure 6-4 and Figure 6-5.

17. Click on the **cps/bps** button on both machines.

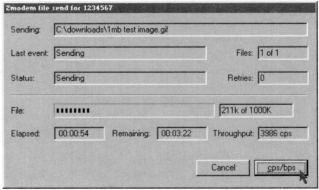

Figure 6-4: HyperTerminal Transmit Operation

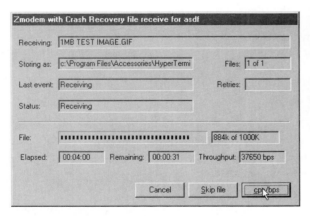

Figure 6-5: HyperTerminal Receive Operation

18. Using Table 6-1, record your observations of the throughput of the client.

19. Record the throughput of the serving computer in Table 6-1 as well.

20. On the client machine, once HyperTerminal indicates that the file transfer has been completed, use the Windows Explorer utility to check the contents of the client's hard drive to be sure that the file *1 MB test image.gif* has been successfully transferred.

21. After locating the file *1 MB test image.gif* in the client's hard drive, rename the file in such a way that the extension of the file now represents the initials of the student(s) running the client.

22. Browse the hard drive on the serving computer and locate the *1 MB test image*.

23. Remove the *1 MB test image* from the server.

24. Once the *1 MB test image* has been deleted from the serving machine check to be sure that the HyperTerminal program is still running on both computers. If it is not, re-establish the connection.

Now the idea is to transfer the file again, this time from the client machine (with the file extension bearing the initials of the client users) to the former server machine. The roles of the two computers will be reversed, however, with the client becoming the server, and the server becoming the client.

25. Beginning with step 12, repeat the procedure through step 22 with the two computers assuming the opposite roles, and the respective data being recorded in Table 6-1 as Server2 and Client2.

26. If necessary, translate the bps/cps data to fill in Table 6-1 by assuming an average of 9 bits per character of data.

27. Once all the data has been entered into Table 6-1, you may terminate the communications session between the server and the client, but do not close the HyperTerminal program.

28. Disconnect the lines running from the phone simulator to both the client machine and the serving machine.

29. With the HyperTerminal program still running, choose an AT command for your modem chip that displays the statistics of the last connection.

The information as to which commands can be used should be supplied in the Users Guide for the modem used in the client PC.

Figure 6-6 contains an example of typical upload and download rates for a modem. Notice that the AT command used to display the statistics for this modem was ati6. TX in the figure is the transmit, or upload rate while RX is the receive, or download rate.

```
OK
ati6
Texas Instruments RK 33600 Fax Link Diagnostics...

Chars sent              6383     Chars Received          18576
Chars lost                 0
Octets sent             3328     Octets Received          6050
Blocks sent              189     Blocks Received           128
Blocks resent              0

Retrains Requested         0     Retrains Granted            0
Line Reversals             0     Blers                       0
Link Timeouts              0     Link Naks                   0

Data Compression     V42BIS 2048/32
Equalization         Long
Fallback             Disabled
Protocol             LAPM
Speed                31200/28800
Last Call            00:02:48
```

Figure 6-6: Transfer Statistics

Keep in mind that although you actually conducted two transfer sessions, the statistics being displayed will correspond only to the most recent file transfer.

Figure 6-7 shows the statistics screen for a Rockwell chipset using the AT command at&v1

To provide effective data for network maintenance purposes, download rates should be measured on several computers at different times of the day. However, due to the time constraints within the classroom environment, the information gathered during the period of time used during this Lab Procedure will have to suffice.

30. From the information gathered during this Lab Procedure, determine which machine, client or server, achieved the highest transfer rate.

31. Determine whether there was a transfer rate discrepancy between the rates reported for the server and its client during a file transfer.

```
at&v1
TERMINATION REASON..........DTR LOSS
LAST TX rate...............................26400 bps
HIGHEST TX rate.......................26400 bps
LAST RX rate..............................26400 bps
HIGHEST RX rate.......................26400 bps
PROTOCOL ................................NONE
COMPRESSION ..........................NONE
Line QUALITY ............................127
Rx LEVEL...................................L053
Highest Rx State ..........................67
Highest TX State ..........................67
EQM Sum....................................007F
RBS Pattern ................................FF
Rate Drop....................................FF
Digital Pad ..................................None
Local Rtrn Count ..........................01
Remote Rtrn Count.......................00
V8bis K56Flex .............................not successful
```

Figure 6-7: Rockwell Display Screen

TABLES

Table 6-1: Server vs. Client Throughput

SERVER/CLIENT THROUGHPUT COMPARISONS		
MACHINE	BPS	CPS
Server/Upload		
Client/Download		
Server2/Upload		
Client2/Download		

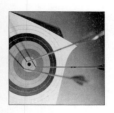

Feedback

LAB QUESTIONS

1. Summarize the results of the upload/download data in Table 6-1.
2. What are several factors that may affect data transfer rates using modems?
3. Why should you choose a compressed file when measuring modem data rates?

Installing, Setting Up, and Testing an NIC

OBJECTIVES

1. Install the network card into a PC expansion slot of a client computer.
2. Determine NIC parameters such as I/O port address, IRQ, and the base memory address.
3. Document all changes as well as any baseline data on the NIC.
4. Use Windows installation software to install and configure a client NIC.
5. Install the cable and document all network connections on a classroom network.

Software Exploration

RESOURCES

1. Network+ Certification Training Guide
2. Windows 2000 Professional workstation
3. PnP Ethernet Network Interface Card (NIC)
4. CAT5 UTP cable with R-J45 connectors
5. NIC vendor documentation and drivers
6. LAN connection

Hardware Exploration

DISCUSSION

This lab describes how to configure and install a network card, and how to connect it into the network. The network card allows the PC to communicate with other computers by way of the network cabling. To install the network, you will need a network card, cables, and connectors.

A portion of the installation process involves configuring the network card. Configuring the card means that numbers are assigned to the card enabling it to communicate with the PC microprocessor. Most network cards are preconfigured with default settings. Refer to the card documentation for the default settings. If possible, use default settings when setting up the network.

When you configure the card depends on the type of card used. Some cards require the user to manipulate jumpers or dip switches on the card. If you use this type of card, refer to the card documentation to determine whether you need to set the switches.

Newer types of NICs are configured after the card is installed using the network software. With these types of cards, configuration is completed during the network software installation. Again, the card documentation will provide instructions.

Manually configuring the card is accomplished with jumper and DIP switches. Figure 7-1(a) shows jumper switches while Figure 7-1(b) illustrates DIP switch changes. To change a jumper setting, remove the plastic hood over the pin on the jumper block. Place the hood on the pins as indicated on the network card documentation. Figure 7-1(a) shows a jumper setting changed from position 2 to position 5.

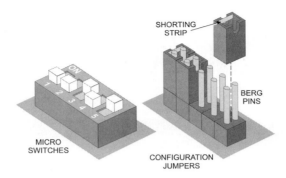

Figure 7-1: Configuration Jumpers and DIP Switches

To reset a DIP switch to an alternate setting (on to off, closed to open, etc.), move the switch to the position indicated in the network documentation. The following sections examine the more common configuration settings and requirements.

When the network card sends a request to the computer's microprocessor, it issues an interrupt (IRQ) to get its attention. Many devices in a computer use unique interrupt request lines, which are assigned during the configuration process.

Software Exploration

PROCEDURE

Generally, IRQ 3/serial port 2 and IRQ 5/parallel port can be used. Plug and Play, however, will automatically locate an available IRQ and install the network card there. To explore the IRQs in Windows 2000:

1. Right-click on the **My Computer** icon and select the **Properties** option.

2. Select the **Hardware** tab and click on the **Device Manager** button.

3. Click on **View** and select the **Resources by type** option.

4. Expand the Interrupt Request (IRQ) item.

5. The IRQs and corresponding devices will be displayed as shown in Figure 7-2.

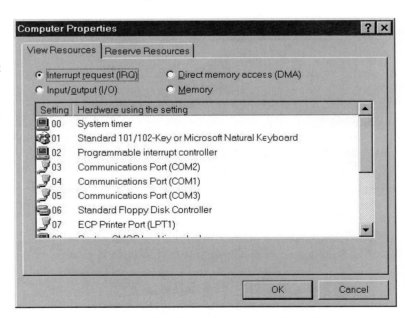

Figure 7-2: Computer Properties Dialog Box

If an interrupt isn't listed, no device will be shown for that IRQ. From the *Device Manager* window, you can also view the DMA, I/O, and memory assignments for various devices installed on the client machine.

Figure 7-3 lists interrupts used with xx286 and higher microprocessors. If your computer doesn't have specific hardware listed for a specific IRQ, that interrupt should be available.

Figure 7-3: Standard Hardware Interrupt Assignments

ASSIGNMENTS FOR HARDWARE INTERRUPTS	
Interrupt #	**Hardware Assignment**
2 (9)	Enhanced/Video Graphics Adapter
3	Available—unless used for a Mouse
4	COM 1 or COM 3 Serial Ports
5	Available
6	Floppy Disk Controller
7	Parallel Port
8	Realtime Clock
10	Available
11	Available
12	Mouse (PS/2)
13	Math CoProcessor
14	Hard Disk Controller
15	Available

The base input/output (I/O) port specifies a channel through which information is transferred between your network card and the computer microprocessor. The port appears to the microprocessor as an address.

Each hardware device in your system must have a different base I/O port number. The port numbers listed in Figure 7-4 are generally available for assignment to the network card. Use Device Manager to view these on any client computer. Those with a device listed next to them are addresses commonly used for PCs and other devices to determine which addresses are in use.

6. Record the available port and IRQ information for later use in Table 7-1, and prepare to physically install the Network Interface Card (NIC).

Figure 7-4: Standard Hardware Port Addresses

PORT ADDRESSES FOR STANDARD HARDWARE	
PORT ADDRESS (HEX)	**DEVICE**
200-20F	Games Port
210-21F	*
220-22F	*
230-23F	Bus Mouse
240-24F	*
250-25F	*
260-26F	*
270-27F	LPT 3
280-28F	*
290-29F	*
2A0-2AF	*
2B0-2BF	*
2C0-2CF	*
2D0-2DF	*
2E0-2EF	*
2F0-2FF	COM 2
300-30F	*
310-31F	*
320-32F	Hard Disk Controller
330-33F	*
340-34F	*
350-35F	*
360-36F	*
370-37F	LPT 2
380-38F	*
390-39F	*
3A0-3AF	*
3B0-3BF	LPT 1
3C0-3CF	EGA/VGA
3D0-3DF	CGA/MCGA/EGA/VGA
3E0-3EF	*

*Not used.

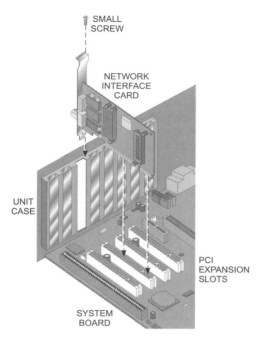

SMALL SCREW

NETWORK INTERFACE CARD

UNIT CASE

PCI EXPANSION SLOTS

SYSTEM BOARD

Figure 7-5: Identifying Expansion Slots

7. Before placing the NIC into the computer, turn off its power and unplug the power cord.

8. Remove the cover from the system unit and identify an expansion slot into which you plan to install the card.

Refer to Figure 7-5 and identify the type of slot your card will use.

9. Remove the NIC from the antistatic bag, ground yourself (using the antistatic wrist strap), and install the network card.

10. Replace the cover of the computer and turn on the power.

As the computer boots, Windows should detect the newly installed NIC.

If the card is detected, you may be offered a dialog box asking if you want to install it. Otherwise, Windows will install it automatically using its own drivers.

11. If you are prompted to supply drivers for the device, insert the disk with the drivers and follow the prompts.

12. Finish the installation if you are prompted.

NOTE: The card is now installed and ready for use with Windows 2000. With the network card configured and installed it's time to install and connect the cables.

13. First, sketch a floorplan showing the location of all the computers that will be on the network.

14. Next, sketch the cable runs and assign a numerical designation to each connection.

Space has been set aside in Figure 7-6 to be used for your sketch.

15. Determine the type of cabling to be used in the network, and record the results in Table 7-2.

Include cable identifying numbers on your sketch, such as CAT5. If, in the future, more PCs are added to the network, the cable type must remain consistent throughout.

16. Physically connect the port of the network card to the network cable. If necessary, refer to Lab Procedure 1 for connections of various cabling schemes.

The specifics of the connection vary with the cable. In this network, all connections will be taken to one of the ports of a multiport hub. Because unshielded twisted pair cabling is being used, and the topology is a star, your cable labeling scheme should denote both ends of the connection.

If this were a bus topology, the last PC at each end of a bus network would have a terminating resistor installed. The resistor would load the cable and prevent data signals from reflecting back through the network.

Figure 7-6: Floorplan of a Classroom Network Exercise

17. Check all connections for a proper fit, and examine solder joints, if applicable, for clean, shiny connections.

18. If you installed new cable and added end-connectors (RJ-45), check for proper polarities using a cable tester.

TABLES

Table 7-1

Port Information	
IRQ Information	

Table 7-2

LAB QUESTIONS

1. How are NICs differentiated on a network?
2. Why is it necessary to assign the network card a unique interrupt?
3. If a network card has no configuration switches, how is it configured?
4. If a list of assigned I/O ports is not available, how can the assignments be determined?
5. Explain why it's important to document the parameters of a client computer.

Feedback

Configuring Windows Peer-to-Peer LANs

Networking

OBJECTIVES

1. Locate the network configuration screens used with Windows 2000.
2. Describe the difference between a peer-to-peer and a server-based LAN.
3. Configure a workstation with a unique computer name.
4. Configure a workstation with a Network layer protocol.
5. Configure a workstation for file and print sharing.
6. State an advantage and a disadvantage of NetBEUI and TCP/IP.

RESOURCES

1. Network+ Certification Training Guide
2. Two Windows 2000 Professional workstations
3. An installed and configured NIC in each workstation

DISCUSSION

Networks that use clients connected to servers are the predominant network type in use today for medium- and large-scale networking. However, many networks consist of ten or less computers connected together in a small business or home office. These networks (sometimes called SOHO, for small office/home office) don't need the powerful features of a network server. Instead, the computers are tied together in a peer-to-peer network.

In a peer-to-peer network, all workstations operate as both clients and servers. In a typical situation, five computers are networked and all users on the network are able to access files on each of the other computers. Imagine a small business in which sales people, bookkeepers, managers, and inventory personnel all need access to information—sometimes the same information. A peer-to-peer LAN may be a good choice for this business because it frees the business from having to maintain a complex information system in order to remain competitive.

Figure 8-1 shows a simple peer-to-peer network. Five workstations are connected to a hub via CAT5 UTP with RJ-45 connectors on each end of the wire. The hub is used as a central switch that allows each user to connect to any other computer.

If you think about the arrangement shown in Figure 8-1, you'll realize that at least three fundamental tasks must be performed in setting up a peer-to-peer LAN:

- Configure the networking software on each of the computers.
- Install networking hardware such as the NIC, cabling, and hub. The hub may also require configuring.
- Set up file shares on each of the workstations.

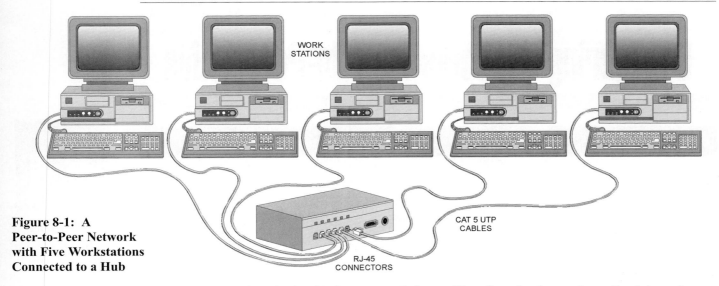

**Figure 8-1: A
Peer-to-Peer Network
with Five Workstations
Connected to a Hub**

Beginning here, and continuing for the next two Labs, you'll perform the three tasks outlined above for a two-station, peer-to-peer LAN. We begin in this Lab by configuring the network software for the workstations. In the next Lab, you'll install the cabling and configure a hub for the network. In Lab 10, you'll manipulate the file shares to cover most of the situations that a user will encounter in a peer-to-peer LAN.

Networking

PROCEDURE

1. Select two computers running Windows 2000 Professional.

NOTE: Both computers must have a Network Interface Card (NIC) installed and configured. If the NIC is not installed and set up, refer to Lab Procedure 7 before continuing.

2. Examine Figure 8-2.

CLIENT TCP/IP SETTINGS			
IP Address Assignment	Automatic?	Yes _____ No _____	
	Specified:	IP _____	Subnet _____
Primary WINS Server IP:			
Secondary WINS Server IP:			
TCP/IP Bindings		Client _____	File/Print Share _____
DNS Entries		Disabled? Yes _____ No _____	
		Host IP _____	
		Domain Name _____	
		DNS Search Order:	
		First: _____ Second: _____ Third: _____ Fourth: _____	

**Figure 8-2: Client
TCP/IP Settings**

Figure 8-2 serves as a configuration documentation form you'll want to complete as you set up and configure the LAN. Recording all of the applicable changes and settings allows you to quickly backtrack your steps to discover the root of any problem that might occur. Not all of the parameters displayed in Figure 8-2 are applicable to a peer-to-peer configuration.

3. Right-click on **My Computer** and select the **Properties** option.

4. Click on the **Network Identification** tab.

The Network Identification tab will appear as shown in Figure 8-3.

5. Click on the **Properties** button.

The *Identification Changes* window, shown in Figure 8-4, will open.

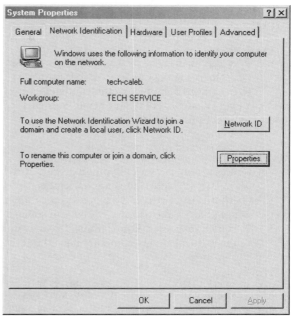

Figure 8-3: Network Properties Folder

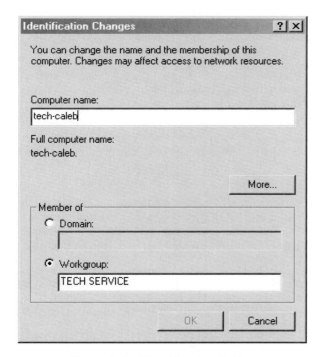

Figure 8-4: Identification Folder

6. In the applicable text boxes, specify a Computer name for each of the two workstations along with a Workgroup name that is common to both.

7. Click on **OK** for the two windows that are open, right-click on **My Network Places**, and select the **Properties** option.

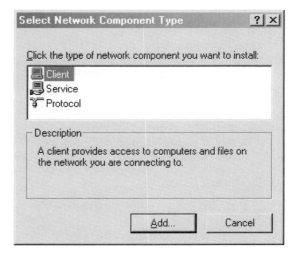

Figure 8-5: Select Network Component Type Dialog Box

8. Right-click on **Local Area Connection** and select the **Properties** option.

9. Click on the **Install** button.

Figure 8-5 is the *Select Network Component Type* dialog box. In addition to specifying network clients at this box, you can also use it to specify the network protocol and client services running on the network.

10. Since the Client for Microsoft Networks is already installed, click on **Protocol**.

11. The *Select Network Protocol* box, shown in Figure 8-6, will open.

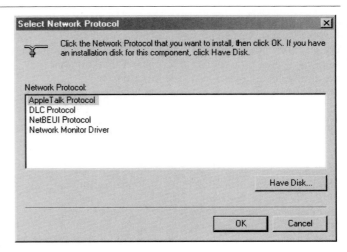

Figure 8-6: Select Network Protocol Box

Notice that there are several Network layer protocols to choose from. In order to connect more than two computers together using Windows 2000, you would normally select from one of these.

In a peer-to-peer LAN using Windows workstations, you have two basic choices concerning networking protocols: NetBEUI or TCP/IP. NetBEUI is a proprietary Microsoft protocol. It's a good choice for small networks because it's easy to set up and maintain. It relies on computer names in order to locate the shared resources. For example, if you want to connect to a file called Networks in a folder called My Documents located on a computer named Internet, NetBEUI will key on the word "Internet" when locating the file.

There are, however, a couple of disadvantages to NetBEUI. To begin with, its simplicity is a huge disadvantage if users on the network will be connecting to other networks. NetBEUI isn't routable; that is, packets using the protocol can't be sent to other networks. This is because it doesn't contain a mechanism for reconciling physical MAC addresses to the name of the computer.

Another disadvantage of NetBEUI is that workstations gain access to the network by responding to queries issued by all other stations. This is called a broadcast, and if five computers are broadcasting their willingness to receive data frames, then the congestion on the network can be heavy. The result is that the performance of the network will diminish with an increase in the number of users and the volume of traffic.

TCP/IP is the protocol used for large networks, including the Internet, because it contains a means of reconciling addresses of workstations no matter where they're located. The most important aspect of locating a node is its address. On a TCP/IP network, nodes are assigned an Internet Protocol (IP) address, which is a logical, rather than a physical address. The logical IP address can then be reconciled to the physical MAC address of the station that's burned into the station's NIC card.

One disadvantage of TCP/IP is that it requires a higher level of technical competence than NetBEUI and is more difficult to manage. The other disadvantage is that all stations must be assigned a unique logical IP address.

Since each station has a logical as well as a physical address, the volume of traffic on the network is greatly diminished compared to the volume on a NetBEUI network. This can eliminate the broadcast storms that may occur in a NetBEUI LAN. A broadcast storm refers to a situation where so many queries are floating around the network that it becomes difficult to squeeze in a data frame.

At this point in the configuration process, you would normally specify an IP address using the TCP/IP configuration screens of Windows, because the hub you'll be configuring in the next procedure requires an IP address. Given another network, you could install a simple hub (a hub that doesn't support management and configuration) and configure the computers to run NetBEUI. There are various performance tools available with Windows that you can use to determine whether NetBEUI is causing you more problems than it's worth.

At this point, you would install TCP/IP. This protocol should be installed by default.

12. If you need to install TCP/IP, follow the prompts to do so, and return to this point.

13. Click on the **Cancel** button twice to return to *Local Area Connection Properties*.

You should see TCP/IP listed under Components used by the connection.

14. Verify that the *File and Printer Sharing for Microsoft Networks* option is checked, as shown in Figure 8-7.

15. Double-click on the **Internet Protocol (TCP/IP)** component.

The *TCP/IP Properties* window now appears, as shown in Figure 8-8.

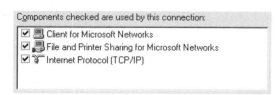

Figure 8-7: Print and File Sharing Box

16. Click on the field labeled *Use the following IP address*:

By selecting this option, you will assign an IP address to the workstation. The other option, Obtain an IP address automatically, is used in a server-based LAN. There are three methods that you can choose from when specifying an IP address. The first method involves purchasing an IP address that is unique in all the world. If the computer will be connecting to the Internet, this is a requirement, because all logical addresses on the Internet must be unique.

If the workstations will connect to the Internet at some time in the future, it's best to secure the IPs now for each of them. Although there are numerous sources for acquiring them, you can start with:

Network Solutions, Inc
505 Huntmar Park Drive
Herndon, VA 22070
703-742-4777

Figure 8-8: TCP/IP Properties/IP Address

The second option is to use test IP addresses that have been reserved for experimental use. This is the option you'll use in this Lab book, unless your instructor has made other plans.

There are three ranges of test IP addresses available. They are:

> 10.x.x.x (Class A range)
> 172.16.x.x-172.31.x.x (Class B range)
> 192.168.x.x (Class C range)

For example, suppose that you choose the first reserved IP address, 10.x.x.x. IP addresses use a dotted decimal notation system for specifying the address. Each "x" represents some decimal number from 1 to 255. You're free to place any number within that range in the place of the x groupings. An example is 10.147.7.16. Another example of a reserved IP is 192.168.24.1.

The third option for assigning IP addresses is to create your own system. Use whatever sequence of numbers you like as long as they follow the dotted decimal system and fall within the range of 1 to 255. For example, you could use 192.32.24.5. If you choose to go this route, keep in mind that an IP in this range is probably assigned to someone, somewhere in the world, and can't be used for experimental purposes across the Internet.

17. With the cursor still located in the "IP Address" field of the *TCP/IP Properties* window, enter an IP address for the first client of **192.168.7.16**.

18. For the second workstation, enter the following IP address: **192.168.7.16**.

19. For each station, enter a subnet mask of **255.255.255.0**.

This means that the first three number sets will be used to identify the network that the stations are on (192.168.7) while the last number set will identify the specific computer (15 and 16). Once you have entered the appropriate information, the IP address section of the TCP/IP Properties dialog box should appear similar to Figure 8-9.

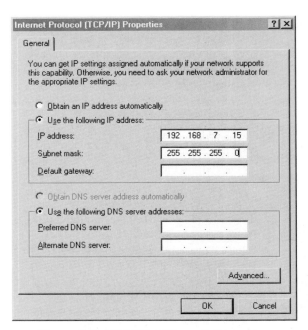

Figure 8-9: TCP/IP Address Information

20. For the remaining areas of the *TCP/IP Properties* and the *Advanced TCP/IP Settings* windows, ensure that they are configured as follows:

- WINS addresses: None
- Gateway: No entries; blank
- DNS Server: None
- Other settings: Default

21. Apply all the settings by clicking on **OK** in any open windows. You may need to restart.

Assigning a Network layer protocol is the minimum requirement for configuring network software settings of a peer-to-peer workstation. While NetBEUI is often a good choice for smaller, peer-to-peer LANs, this procedure used TCP/IP because the hub used in these experiments requires a specific IP address.

Once the hub is configured in the next Lab Procedure, you can test the settings to see if they work properly.

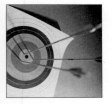

Feedback

LAB QUESTIONS

1. Beginning with the Windows desktop, state the path to the dialog box used for specifying network settings.

2. What is the difference between a peer-to-peer and a server-based LAN?

3. What steps may be followed to select a Network layer protocol for this network?

4. What is one advantage and one disadvantage of NetBEUI?

5. What is one advantage and one disadvantage of TCP/IP?

6. Why was the TCP/IP protocol used in this Lab procedure?

Configuring a Cisco Catalyst 2950 Switch

Networking

OBJECTIVES

1. Recognize the status of port LEDs on the Cisco Catalyst 2950 switch.
2. State the purpose of each connector on the switch.
3. Set up a terminal emulator to access the switch configuration settings.
4. Configure the switch with a unique IP address.
5. Test the functionality of the configuration.
6. Test the switch in a two-workstation, peer-to-peer LAN.

RESOURCES

1. Two workstations configured for file sharing and with unique IP addresses
2. Two CAT5 UTP cables with RJ-45 connectors on each end of the cable
3. One Cisco Catalyst 2950 switch
4. IP address that differs from the IP addresses used in the two workstations

DISCUSSION

In this procedure, you will configure a switch for use in a peer-to-peer LAN. Using the two workstations set up in the previous procedure, you will then use the switch to connect them together, so that files may be shared between the two. In order to configure the switch, you must be able to access and mange the configuration settings, as well as change them when conditions on the network change. This Lab serves as an introduction to a sophisticated switch that will be used in experiments that follow.

The **switch** is a multiport repeater that has 24 10/100BaseT twisted-pair ports for standard computer connections and is compliant to the IEEE 802.3 standard for 10/100BaseT LANs, as well as Ethernet. It also has a console twisted-pair port for configuration.

The switch has the following features:

- When a device is connected and the cables between the device and switch are good, an LED will light on the switch.
- It resends data after a collision on the network.
- It disables individual ports if the connected device does not appear to be working properly. This partitions that device from the rest of the network.

Figure 9-1 shows the front of the switch along with important port connections and status lights. The back of the switch is shown in Figure 9-2.

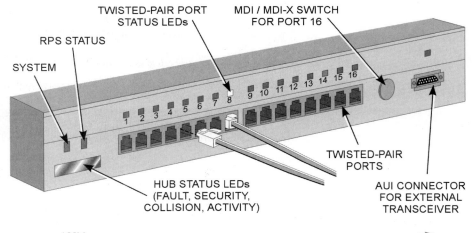

Figure 9-1: Front Panel of the 10/100BaseT Switch

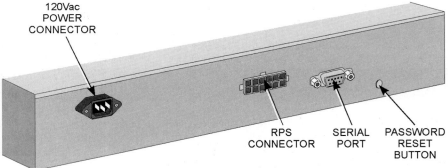

Figure 9-2: Back Panel of the 10/100BaseT Switch

- *10/100BaseT Twisted-pair Ports:* These twisted-pair ports accommodate RJ-45 connectors. While the type of twisted-pair cable is irrelevant to the switch, you will use CAT5 UTP for all experiments in the following procedures.

- *Status LEDs:* The switch comes with a variety of LEDs designed to tell you the operational status of the switch. When the switch is first turned on, it conducts a self-test and the LEDs light in accordance with the outcome of the test. After passing the self-test, the LEDs continue to indicate several network and switch conditions.

During the self-test, all the port lights stay on for a second. The switch is running its POST self-tests to make sure it is working properly. Once the switch passes the test, it is ready for use in a normal environment; but if it does not pass the self-test, recycle power several times to try and clear the fault condition. The switch does not have an ON/OFF switch, so recycle the power by unplugging it from the AC source or redundant power supply.

Figure 9-3 shows the state of the port status LEDs after passing the self-test. Note that the port LEDs remain unlit until a connection is made from an Ethernet or IEEE802.3 compliant device. The presence of a lit port does not mean that the connected device (a NIC, for example) is working properly, or that the PC it is installed in can access the switch. It merely means that the cable is good and that the connected device is compliant to one of the standards.

The switch uses the RPS (Redundant Power Supply) connector to attach the switch to a backup power source. If the main power fails, the RPS will continue to supply power to the switch.

PORT STATUS LEDS AFTER PASSING SELF-TEST	
State	Meaning of LED
Off	System is not powered up.
Green	System is operating normally.
Amber	System is receiving power but not functioning properly.

Figure 9-3: Port Status LEDs After Passing Self-Test

A terminal cable is used to access the switch to configure it for a network. A simple switch does not support management. To use a simple switch, apply AC power, and connect the RJ-45 connectors to the switch and PCs. The CISCO switch you will be using is more sophisticated than a simple switch. Before it can be used, it must be properly set up and configured. The terminal port is the connection you will use to access the configuration screens for the switch.

PROCEDURE

Networking

The Catalyst 2950 10/100BaseT switch must first be configured before it is ready to use. The manufacturer ships the switch with a default set of configuration parameters that must be manipulated before it can be used in an actual network. In order to configure and manage the switch, you must set up an ASCII console session with it. We do this by connecting the switch to a PC running a terminal emulator program.

The terminal emulator you will use is "HyperTerminal," available on Windows 2000 Professional workstations. The switch comes with a crossover RJ-45 cable, and an RJ-45 to DB-8 serial adapter.

The serial port connectors available on the back of personal computers vary widely. Typically, there are two connectors: One is a 9-pin connector and the other is a 25-pin connector. The serial adapter that comes with the switch is the 9-pin variety. If you do not have a free 9-pin serial port on your computer, you can get a DB-9 to DB-25 adapter at any electronics store.

1.   Connect the cable from a PC to the switch.

2.   Navigate to Start/Programs/Accessories/Communications/HyperTerminal.

3.   When HyperTerminal's *Connection Description* box appears, enter a unique name for your configuration session.

Notice that you also have a choice as to which icon you wish to use to identify the session file you are about to make.

4.   Click on the **OK** button.

The *Connect To* dialog box will open, as shown in Figure 9-4.

Because you will not be dialing into the switch, no phone number will be entered. Instead, you will use a COM port of the PC. Your mouse may use COM port 1, unless you are using a ps2 or USB mouse, in which case COM1 should be free. But in either case, you should have access to COM2.

5.   In the *Connect Using* field, choose either **COM1** or **COM2**, depending on availability. Ask your instructor if you are not sure.

Figure 9-4: Connect To Dialog Box of HyperTerminal

6. Click on the **OK** button, and the *COM Properties* dialog box, shown in Figure 9-5, will open.

7. Adjust the settings to match the settings in Figure 9-5, and click on the **OK** button.

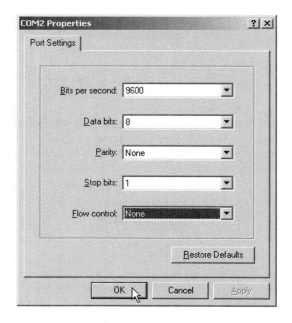

Figure 9-5: COM2 Properties Dialog Box

Any COM port conflicts will cause an error warning that the selected COM port could not be opened. At this point, you must resolve the conflict. If another device is using the port, it must be removed/switched or you will not be able to access the switch.

8. When the *HyperTerminal* screen appears, click on the **File** menu item, and select **Properties**.

A dialog box similar to the previous one appears, as shown in Figure 9-6. Here an important parameter is found under the *Settings* tab, in the *Emulation* field. Leaving this at *Auto detect* should work fine, but if you have trouble, use the scroll bar and choose **VT100**.

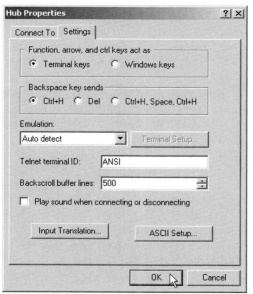

9. Click on the **OK** button to return to the terminal screen.

You should see a blank terminal screen. Now you must power up the switch so that you can configure it.

Figure 9-6: Session Properties Dialog Box

10. Connect the AC power cord to the back of the unit, and plug it into a grounded, 120Vac outlet.

After a few seconds, the terminal screen should start displaying text, as shown in Figure 9-7. This text is showing the POST tests that the switch is running. After the tests are done, you will be asked the following question: *Would you like to enter the initial configuration dialog?*

11. Type **yes** to begin initial configuration. You will be confronted with the following question: *Would you like to enter basic management setup?*

12. Type **yes** to enter basic management setup.

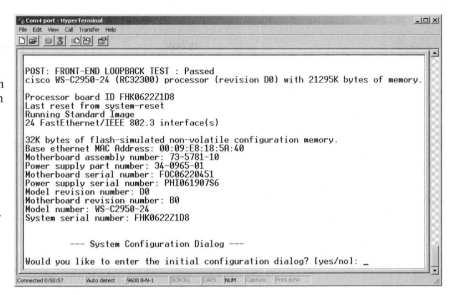

Figure 9-7: Initial Console Screen of the CISCO Catalyst 2950 10/100BaseT Switch

13. When asked for a hostname, enter the name **hostswitch**, and write it down in Table 9-1.

14. When asked for an enable secret, enter the password, **marcraft**, and write it down in Table 9-1.

15. When asked for an enable password, enter the password, **tech**, and write it down in Table 9-1.

16. When asked for a virtual terminal password, enter the password, **virtual**, and write it down in Table 9-1.

17. When asked *Configure SNMP Network Management*, enter **no** and press the **ENTER** key.

Now the screen will display all the interfaces in the switch. Press a key whenever it says —*more*— at the bottom of the screen to continue through the list.

18. When asked to enter the interface name, enter **Vlan1**, and press the **ENTER** key.

19. When asked if you would like to configure IP on that interface, enter **yes** and press the **ENTER** key.

20. Now specify an IP address to assign to the switch. Ask your instructor for the IP address and write it down in Table 9-1.

21. When asked for a subnet mask, enter **255.255.255.0**, and press the **ENTER** key.

22. When asked if you would like to enable as a cluster command switch, enter **no**, and press the **ENTER** key.

It will now show the configuration script it generated from your answers. Press a key whenever it says —*more*— at the bottom of the screen to continue through the list.

23. When confronted with the question *Enter your selection [2]*, enter **2** and press the **Enter** key to save the configuration and exit.

When you are prompted with *Press RETURN to get started!* you are done configuring the switch. You need to test it to determine if it can communicate with the clients.

24. Check to make sure that the power has first been turned off on the client machines and the switch.

25. Connect a CAT5 UTP cable—with RJ-45 connectors on each end—to the NIC in each of the clients, and to any two of the 10/100BaseT ports on the switch.

26. Turn on power to the switch, then the two computers.

27. Navigate to *Start/Run*, type **cmd.exe** at the prompt, and click on the **OK** button.

Now we will use the TCP/IP utility PING. Ping is used to send test packets to a specified address, and then listen for an echo of these same packets from the destination. If the packets are returned, it means that the connection from the switch to the destination is working. To run Ping, you enter the IP address of the destination, which will be one of the client computers.

28. Type **Ping XXX.XXX.XXX.XXX** where the X's are replaced by the IP address of the other client computer. Fore example, Ping 192.168.0.22. Press the **ENTER** key to run Ping.

NOTE: If you receive a message that says "Request Timed Out," then there is no connection to the other computer. Verify that you typed the correct IP address.

29. If the switch is properly configured, you will see the packets echoed back on your screen. This tells you that a channel exists from client to client through the switch.

With the switch configured as in this procedure, you connected 24 client computers to share information in a peer-to-peer network—a relatively easy network to set up and maintain. However, the Catalyst 2950 10/100BaseT switch has far more features than will ever be needed for a peer-to-peer network. We will explore many of these features in the remaining procedures.

The Catalyst 10/100BaseT switch also remains a good choice for a simple network, because it provides for future growth. The most serious drawback to using the switch is that it requires IP addresses, something that a small network does not need. But the clients will not be connecting to the Internet through the switch, you can assign them test IP addresses, or create your own addressing scheme.

TABLES

Table 9-1: Switch Settings

SWITCH SETTINGS	
Host name	
Enable Secret	
Enable Password	
Virtual Terminal Password	
IP Address	

LAB QUESTIONS

Feedback

1. Why is HyperTerminal used in this procedure?
2. To configure this switch for a peer-to-peer LAN, what settings must you configure?
3. What TCP/IP utility is used to test the link from switch to workstation?
4. What values must be configured to test the link from switch to workstation?

Sharing Files in a Peer-to-Peer LAN

OBJECTIVES

1. Add a new user account to test permission-based user-level share access.
2. Set up a share on a folder.
3. Connect to a shared network resource.
4. Set up drive mapping to a folder on another computer.
5. Test all file shares.

Operating System Technology

RESOURCES

1. Network+ Certification Training Guide
2. Two Windows 2000 Professional workstations
3. CISCO 10BaseT hub configured with an IP address

DISCUSSION

In the previous two lab procedures, you set up the networking configuration for two workstations and configured a hub with an IP address. The basic elements are now in place to share files between workstations on the LAN. In this Lab Procedure, you will configure the workstations for file sharing.

User-level access control means that access is granted based upon access privileges granted to a single user or a group of users. This type of sharing is typically employed in a server-based LAN.

In order to set up sharing, you have two tasks to perform:

- Specify shares on a workstation.

- Connect to resources on another workstation that have been designated as shared.

You will use user-level access control in this experiment. To do so, you will need to create test files on both workstations and save them in a directory. Then, you'll configure the files for sharing.

To test the network, you will connect to the shared files on another workstation and view them. Sharing will be extended so that, ultimately, all resources on either computer can be accessed from another computer.

Before beginning, review Lab Procedure 8 to make sure that the computers have been configured with TCP/IP, Client For Microsoft Networks, and that File and Print Sharing is enabled.

**Operating
System
Technology**

PROCEDURE

1. From the desktop of one of the two workstations, navigate the *Start/Settings/Control Panel/Administrative Tools* path and open the Computer Management console.

   Computer Management is one of the main administrative tools that are used in Windows 2000. Although it is used briefly here, it will be covered more in depth during Lab Procedure 15.

2. After Computer Management has loaded, it should appear similar to Figure 10-1. In the *Tree* pane to the left, click through the *Computer Management/System Tools/Local Users and Groups/Users* path.

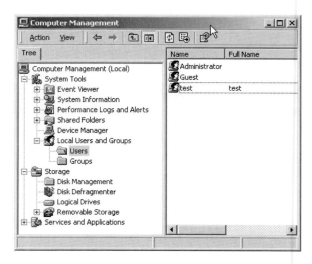

Figure 10-1: Computer Management

3. With the *Users* folder highlighted in the *Tree* pane, click through the *Action/New User* path in the menu bar.

4. When the *New User* window pops up, type **test** in the *User name* dialog box.

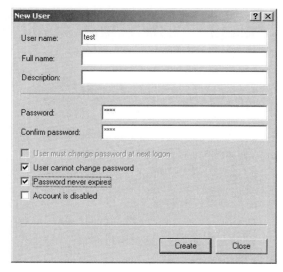

Figure 10-2: Adding a New User

5. Enter **test** in the field named *Password*, and in the *Confirm password* field.

6. Clear the *User must change password at next logon* checkbox and enable the **User cannot change password** option.

7. Something similar to Figure 10-2 should be on your screen. Click on the **Create** button, then the **Close** button, then close the *Computer Management* window.

8. Now double-click on the **My Computer** icon.

9. Then, double-click on the icon representing **drive C**.

10. From the drive C menu bar, navigate the *File/New/Folder* path.

11. Locate the *new* folder and highlight it.

12. Click in the *new folder's* name box, and rename it by typing **temp**. Then, press **ENTER** to continue.

Because you are creating a folder for use with this specific procedure, do not utilize any folder that already employs the name *temp*. If such a situation exists on your C drive, name the new folder *TEMP2*.

13. Double-click on the **temp** folder you just created.

14. From the *temp* folder window, navigate the *File/New/Text Document* path.

15. Click on the new text document file to highlight it. Then, click once inside its name box.

16. For its new name, type **Test_1xxx.txt**, and press the **ENTER** key.

Substitute your initials for the *xxx* part of the filename to differentiate your file from those of other students who may use the same workstation.

17. Still in the *temp* folder window, double-click on the icon for **Test_1xxx.txt**.

18. When the *Notepad* (or other word processor) screen appears, create some text in the empty file.

It would be a good idea to identify yourself, your lab partner, your class, the date and time, and the name of your workstation using the text you type in. You may include other information as well.

19. When you have finished typing, **Save** the file and **Close** the word processor (*Notepad*, etc.).

20. From the *temp* folder, click on the **Up** tool button just below the Menu bar to move up one directory.

21. As the group assigned to the second computer performs steps 9 through 20 for their workstation, check with them to be sure that they type **Test_2xxx.txt** for the new filename in step 17.

It really doesn't matter which filename is selected for which computer, as long as each workstation uses a different name for identification of its text file. Also, be sure to keep track of the computer name of each workstation. After the files have been created, you can specify the share access properties.

22. At the *C:\ drive* window, click on the **temp** folder.

Because new folders are normally placed at the bottom of the window, you may need to scroll down to it.

23. From the *File* entry in the drop-down menu, choose the **Sharing** option. The *Sharing* dialog box for *temp Properties*, shown in Figure 10-3, will open.

Sharing is also available through the *Properties* page of the drop-down File menu, or by right-clicking the folder and choosing the **Sharing** option.

If the Sharing option doesn't appear in the menu, check to make sure that you have File and Print Sharing in the Network Properties, as discussed in Procedure 8.

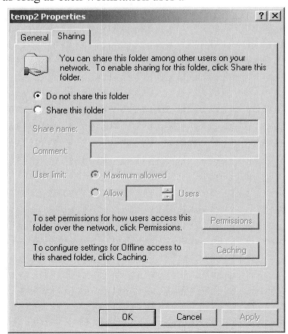

Figure 10-3: Folder Sharing Properties

24. Click in the field marked **Share this folder**.

25. In the *Share name* field, enter the name of the folder, if it has not already been named.

26. Click on the **Permissions** button.

27. In the *Name* field highlight the **Everyone** entry and click on the **Remove** button.

The "Everyone" user encompasses all users and groups, and enables them to access that share. In this example, the share is meant to be accessed by only one user. However, the "Everyone" user could be helpful in some networking situations.

28. Now, click on the **Add** button.

29. In the *Name* field of the *Select Users, Computers,* or *Groups* window, scroll down to find the account called **test**. Select it, click on the **Add** button below it, and then click on the **OK** button.

30. In the *Permissions* pane on the *Permissions for temp* window, select the **Allow Full Control** field. It should select all of the *Allow* fields. Click on the **OK** button.

31. Click on the **OK** button in the *temp Properties* window and check to be sure that sharing has been set up for both the *test_1xxx.txt* and *test_2xxx.txt* files on both workstations, and that each computer has a new test user. Close all windows.

Note that Windows provides three levels of permission security for shares: Full Access, Change, and Read. *Read* means that another user can read or execute a file but isn't permitted to change it. *Change* allows a user to write to, and change attributes of shared files, as well as do everything the Read permission allows. *Full* means that a user can delete, take ownership of, and change permissions of shared files, as well as do everything the Change permission allows.

In sharing access to the subdirectory where the test file is located, you have opened up access to all contents of the folder.

32. Log out of each computer by navigating the *Start/Shut Down* path, and choosing the **Log Off** option in the drop-down menu.

33. Click on the **Yes** button to exit.

34. When the *Logon* screen appears, press the **CTRL+ALT+DEL** keys if the system prompts you.

35. In the *User Name* field, type **test**. Also type **test** into the *Password* field.

36. Make sure that the *Log on using dial-up connection* field isn't selected, and then click on the **OK** button.

37. After the *test* desktop has loaded, double-click on the **My Network Places** icon.

38. After the *My Network Places* window has loaded, double-click on the **Computers Near Me** icon.

The computers that are in the workgroup of your computer will appear on the screen. Figure 10-4 shows an example of this.

39. Double-click on the network name of the other group's computer.

40. In the next window, you should see a shared folder named *temp*. Double-click on it and open the applicable test file.

At this point, you should be able to verify the operation of the peer-to-peer LAN you've set up. If you can access files on the other computer, the setup has been successful. Notice that what you've done is to share a subdirectory on another computer in order to have access to its files. This level of sharing may be all that's needed for some situations.

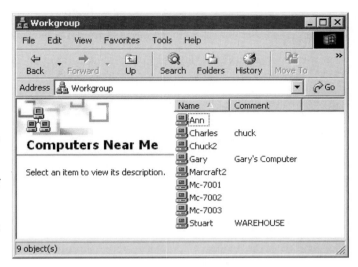

Figure 10-4: Computers Near Me

41. Close all open windows.

In other situations, you may need to set up more than one folder for sharing. When this occurs, simply repeat the previous steps for each share. Keep in mind that you must first share the folder on a computer before you can connect to it.

Alternatively, a complete directory, such as C:, can be set up for sharing. The steps for doing so are identical to these. Select the drive from the computer where it's to be shared, give it a name and set up permissions, then connect to it from another computer.

To connect to a document on another computer, you can click on its computer icon in My Network Places, and navigate through subdirectories until you get to the file you want. Alternately, you can map a drive letter to the resource. This is nothing more than establishing a shortcut to resources on another computer. The advantage of mapping drives is that it saves time.

42. Navigate through My Network Places to the temp share on the other computer.

43. Right-click on the temp share folder, and select the **Map Network Drive** option from the pop-up menu.

The *Map Network Drive* dialog box, shown in Figure 10-5, appears.

44. Choose any unused drive letter, and close the *Map Network Drive* dialog box by clicking on the **Finish** button.

The window for the mapped drive appears, showing the files and folders that are currently available at the mapped drive location.

Figure 10-5: Mapping A Network Drive

45. Close the *Map Network Drive* window and check to see if you're connected by double-clicking on **My Computer** from the desktop.

The new drive letter, and its name, will be shown in the listing along with an appropriate icon.

46. Double-click on the **temp drive letter** icon.

The remote subdirectory should open on your screen. (This is actually the same window that opened when you first mapped the drive.)

47. Close the windows to the mapped drive.

The entire contents of a hard drive can be shared if it is set up properly. Simply repeat steps 1-47, and use the root directory (C:, or another drive) as the share. If you employ specific user permissions, make sure that the users are identical on both computers.

A peer-to-peer LAN is an excellent choice for small networks used in home-based businesses, or small offices. It allows users to share files without the complexity that a server would bring to the network. Once the network operating system is installed, and the physical hardware is installed and configured, shares must be set up on the workstations.

It's somewhat ironic that setting up shares can often be the most tedious part of a network install. The reason is that you're designing the working environment for someone else. In many cases, a supervisor or manager may dictate share access. This can get rather convoluted, particularly when the affected user doesn't agree with the supervisor. It often involves a bit of diplomacy, educating both the supervisor and the employee to the practicalities of sharing resources.

Feedback

LAB QUESTIONS

1. Describe the steps needed to establish a share on a file called *Literature* that is located in a folder called *Information* and has Read permissions to everyone.
2. Describe the steps needed to map a drive letter to the folder called *Literature* that's located on a computer called BOB.
3. What are the three permission security levels available for sharing with Windows 2000 Professional?
4. A user has a folder that needs to be shared with five other users. However, only two of them are to be able to modify the contents of the folder. The remaining three are permitted only to read the contents of the folder. Describe how you will handle this situation.

Planning a Network Installation

OBJECTIVES

1. Discuss how planning a network design affects the efficiency and effectiveness of the network.
2. Given a specification sheet for a network, create a formal design.

**Planning
Strategy**

RESOURCES

1. Network+ Certification Training Guide
2. Windows 2000 Hardware Compatibility List
3. Network component resources such as catalogues, web pages, etc.

DISCUSSION

A basic understanding of the issues surrounding planning is as important as understanding the difference between a router and an NIC card. This is because a network is far more likely to run inefficiently and ineffectively if it isn't well planned. This Lab Procedure is a prelude to the Windows 2000 installation you'll perform in the next experiment. The decisions you must make during the installation will be resolved here, as well as some other important decisions.

If you're the network administrator and the network suffers frequent outages that could have been prevented with a sound implementation plan, then you're the one who gets blamed when it crashes. There are some very good reasons for planning an installation. The most important one is the business goals of a company. Networks are expensive and indispensable—they're a required tool that can cost a lot of money to install and maintain. You simply can't afford to make too many bad decisions, and expect to keep your job.

If the network isn't planned, the cost to maintain it will be high. As an example, you need to plan a network for future growth. If a hub is slated for a LAN with eight users, you would not buy a hub with eight ports; rather, you'd buy a 16- or 24-port hub. If a ninth user is added to the LAN, then you'll have to replace the 8-port hub. It's easier to get the money in the design stage for the more expensive hub than it is to go to a manager in six months to say that the equipment they recently approved is now out of date.

Along with economics—which is always a balancing act between what's nice to have, and what's needed—are other important issues. The network operating system, needs of users, application software that will be running, Network layer protocols, and server file systems are all important decisions that must be made before any equipment is ordered.

Table 11-1 is a checklist that contains most of the points that should be considered in the network design stage. Once you have a workable design, prepare a sketch of the network showing the location of all hardware components. Use the sketch when talking with users and supervisors to determine the best location of equipment such as printers. Next, it's time to source equipment and software. This stage includes pricing and expected delivery times. Since you'll have a budget to work within, the prices must conform to the budget. Generally, if the cost of a project exceeds the initial budget, it's a strike against you.

While you can summarize some of the hardware and software on a network, you can't do it thoroughly until you've canvassed personnel who will be using the network. They have different needs and expectations of a network. Make sure that the hardware and software you've identified will be compatible with equipment they're using, and in some cases, with network components they are already working with.

Servers have their own requirements, and we'll take a detailed look at these during the Lab. Software running on clients needs to be compatible with network protocols and the server operating system. Again, make sure you have a detailed understanding of what the user's needs are.

PROCEDURE

Planning Strategy

1. Refer to the LAN description in Figure 11-1.

This will be the basic blueprint from which you'll plan and design a network.

LAN Specification Sheet

A LAN is required to support five workstations. The workstations will be using Windows 2000 operating system with Microsoft Office Suite and Corel WordPerfect Office Suite, as well as several desktop publishing programs such as Adobe Acrobat and Front Page Web editor. The users on the LAN will be preparing documentation that includes numerous text and graphical files for paper-printed products, web-based applications, and documentation that will be placed on CDs.

Because much of their work is done concurrently, each user needs access to files on the other computers as well as a central storage site where user files are routinely backed up.

At this time, none of the users have access to the Internet or e-mail, but they will within the next six months.

The company has numerous isolated groups such as this one, and plans to link them into a large, segmented LAN over the next year.

The company uses many legacy systems but is attempting to convert most of them to Microsoft products for client and network operating systems, and to utilize CISCO hardware wherever possible. Some groups, however, run UNIX machines and are connected to UNIX servers, and this isn't likely to change. The NOS (Network Operating System) chosen for this particular group must be compatible with UNIX software.

LAN servers used on small networks will be connected to a high-speed server farm that runs across the wire at 100 Mbps. The cabling infrastructure selected for this LAN, as well as NICs, must be capable of achieving 100 Mbps data rates.

The budget for this project is $10,000, and the project itself must be completed in 40 working hours. The budgeted hourly rate for work is $75/hour. A basic design concept must be approved before the equipment is ordered and the installation is scheduled.

Figure 11-1: Network Specification Description

2. For the first step, assume that the client operating systems are in place and are running Windows 2000 Professional.

3. Next, assume that the Network Operating System (NOS) will be Windows 2000, because the company is trying to standardize on Microsoft products.

4. Now, draw a simple sketch of the network in the space provided in Figure 11-2.

Show only the hardware and operating systems in the sketch, including the floor plan, cabling scheme, and component identification for a five-client, server-based LAN.

Figure 11-2: Sketch of Proposed Network

5. Once you've finished your sketch, have your instructor examine it before continuing.

PROCEDURE - 11

Be certain that your LAN sketch includes the five clients, a server, a hub, and a printer connected to one of the clients. The clients will be running Windows 2000 Professional, and the server will have Windows 2000 Server installed on it.

6. Now, decide on an access method, topology, and wiring infrastructure.

Refer back to Figure 11-1 for hints that will lead you to a good choice.

7. Label the sketch with your recommendations.

The access methods available are Ethernet (CSMA/CD, IEEE 802.3), Token Ring (IEEE 802.5), Token Bus (IEEE 802.4), or, perhaps, VG-AnyLAN. The one that's selected must be capable of 100 Mbps data rates. This eliminates Token Bus and Token Ring. VG-AnyLAN runs at 100 Mbps, but isn't an approved standard yet—so, it's eliminated. That leaves Ethernet as the access method.

Because the topology will be a star configuration, a hub will be required by default.

The wiring infrastructure may be twisted pairs, coaxial cable, fiber optics, or microwaves. Network-grade coaxial has a maximum bandwidth of 10 Mbps, so it's eliminated. The fiber-optic choice will easily handle the high data rate requirement, but the low budget of this LAN will eliminate it. The cabling costs, hub cost, NIC costs, and labor costs will all increase if fiber optics are chosen.

This leaves twisted pairs and microwaves. The cost of a wireless LAN will probably exceed the cost of a copper-based LAN, and the technical expertise required to install, maintain, and support it may not be available in the company. Twisted pair cabling is well-known and understood. It will be the better choice.

What type of twisted pair? Assume the worst and select the best cable—CAT5 UTP.

The type of NICs used in the clients and the server must now be determined. Remember the requirement that all components must be capable of handling 100 Mbps data rates. The server NIC must have a 100 Mbps capability because it connects to the high-speed servers over a 100 Mbps link. The clients will require 10/100 Mbps cards. The 10 Mbps rate will be run across the LAN, but if the speed of the network is increased to 100M, the capability will already be installed.

8. In the space below, list the requirements of a hub for this LAN.

_____

_____

_____

_____

_____

_____

_____

_____

9. Based upon decisions made to this point, as well as the specifications described in Figure 11-1, determine the minimum specifications of the hub.

The hub needs ports for five users and a server, for a total of six ports. A wise decision would be to use one having a minimum of twelve ports. It also needs to support 10 Mbps data rates to the clients, and have a 100 Mbps data rate for a link to the server farm.

There are many varieties of hubs, and the cost of them varies from as little as one hundred, to as much as several thousands of dollars. Some hubs are stand-alones that may or may not be stacked to other hubs. Others are simple (dumb), because their configuration can't be software-managed from a remote terminal. Still others can be managed and configured from any workstation.

Certain hubs are switching types, meaning that they're designed to switch the access to the port connected to the desired channel. This allows the port to use the full bandwidth of the selected channel. Other hubs are chassis-types, containing sixteen or more slots for specialized printed circuit boards that contain Ethernet, Token Ring, fiber optic, management, and a host of other capabilities, including bridging and routing.

Here are some simple guidelines for selecting a hub:

- Select one with twice as many ports as are currently required.

- Select a hub with at least one, and preferably two, specialized uplink ports for fast access. These are typically 100/1000 Mbps Ethernet or fiber optic. If the uplink isn't needed, make sure it can also be used as a normal client port.

- Select a hub that supports management from a workstation. The hub will be—or should be—secured in a locked room. If you have to physically go to the room each time a configuration change is needed, you'll cost your company money, and experience unnecessary aggravation.

- Select the hub from a company that you know and trust, and that has a web site where upgrades may be obtained.

The hub specified for this course (CISCO HP 10BaseT Hub-16M) fits most of these requirements. It's neither a simple or a complex hub, and it would make a good choice for the scenario described in this lab.

Figure 11-3 is a specification sheet for the server used on the LAN. It contains many of the decisions that would need to be made before the Windows NT software could be installed on the server.

10. Review the questions on the server questionnaire for the LAN in Figure 11-3, and use the extra space provided to list any other specifics that you can think of.

This is an extremely important part of designing and planning a network. Mistakes made here can be difficult and expensive to correct once the LAN is installed.

Server Consideration Questionnaire

1. Is Windows 2000 Server compatible with the client OS?
2. Will Windows 2000 Server allow all users access to files that are needed for the publications?
3. Will users be able to have private areas where files won't be shared?
4. Can Windows 2000 be connected to an Ethernet hub?
5. Can Windows 2000 pass data over to a 100 Mbps port on the hub?
6. Which Network protocol will be run on the network, TCP/IP or NetBEUI?
7. Does Windows 2000 support the selected protocol?
8. What type of server disk file system will be used—FAT, NTFS, or both?
9. Does Windows 2000 support the selected file system?
10. Will client workstations be designated as workgroup members, or members of a domain? What will the name of the workgroup or domain be?
11. Which type of access control will be used—share-level or user-level?
12. How will clients be identified—by computer name, IP address, or both?
13. If IP addresses are used, will they be statically assigned to each workstation, or dynamically assigned by the server?
14. Will any type of fault tolerance be used, and will file backups be made to tape or to another server?
15. Will uninterruptible power supplies (UPSs) be used for servers, workstations, and hubs?
16. Will any SCSI devices be installed on the server, and if so, what will they be?
17. What will the mandatory user and optional company names be for the Windows 2000 installation prompts.
18. Which licensing mode will you use—a per-seat or per-server license?
19. What is the unique computer name of the server, not exceeding 15 characters.
20. What type of server will this be—a primary domain controller, or a secondary domain controller?
21. What is the Administrator password?
22. List specifications of the server hardware, including the type/speed of the microprocessor, the number of microprocessors, the type of hard drive (IDE, EIDE, or SCSI), the size of the hard drive, the number of hard drives, the number and type of expansion slots, the amount of RAM, the make and speed of the CD-ROM, and the make of floppy drive.
23. Are the specified peripherals listed on the Windows 2000 Hardware Compatibility List (HCL)?

Figure 11-3: Server Specification Sheet

11. Completely answer as many of the questions regarding the specifications of the server as you can.

Your instructor should be able to provide some information regarding the servers being used in your classroom. Although much of the decision making about the servers has already been made by the education department at your facility, you should become familiar with the various considerations taken into account when determining the specifications that may be required of the server that connects to your workgroup.

12. Once you've finished answering items on the server questionnaire, read the following discussion and discuss various recommendations with your instructor.

Many of the questions posed in Figure 11-3 have been taken into consideration before the classroom network was laid out. Some of them will be dealt with in other Lab Procedures. However, it's best to gather as much information as you can about the server hardware and its basic attributes before beginning an installation. The fewer surprises, the better.

Here are some typical answers to the questions posed:

- Windows 2000 is compatible with all Windows client operating systems, as well as NetWare client software. Sharing files and granting access rights on a network is complex and time consuming, particularly when employees change jobs or turnover rates are high. The answer to both the second and third questions, though, is yes.

- Windows can be connected to an Ethernet hub as well as about any other type of hub. It works best in small- to medium-sized networks, where the number of read/write requests is manageable. The rate that data is passed from a server depends on the NIC, and to a lesser extent, the bus speed of the server board and the mechanics of its hard drive.

- Plan on running both TCP/IP and NetBEUI on the LAN. Initially, you'll set up the LAN for NetBEUI, then change it to TCP/IP and compare the two protocols.

- FAT (File Allocation Table) is the file system used with Windows client operating systems, including Windows 98. NTFS (New Technology File System) is unique to Windows 2000, and isn't directly compatible with FAT. Because this is an exclusive Windows 2000 network, it's best to only configure the hard drive with NTFS.

- You'll set up the clients in a later Lab so that they are members of a domain. The reason is that if they are left as workgroup members, access, passwords, rights, and privileges must be set up for each client individually. When they are a part of a domain, a central account is set up for each user, and stored at the server.

- Clients will be identified by both computer name and IP address. But, initially, only the computer name will be used. Note that for the purposes of this Lab, you would choose IP addresses because this creates the possibility of connecting the clients to the Internet in the future, as well as interconnecting the LAN to other LANs.

No fault tolerance is specified until later in this book. However, check with your instructor.

Check with your instructor for the specifics of the server hardware. Make a list of the specifics, particularly if SCSI devices are used. Review the Windows HCL to make sure that the components can be used with Windows 2000.

More than likely, you'll specify a per-server license agreement. Again, check with your instructor.

You'll need approval from your instructor for a computer name and an Administrator password for the server. Client passwords should also be approved by your instructor.

13. Create a final design for the network described in this Lab. Incorporate the information you've gathered into the plan. Include a list of costs, sources for the materials and equipment, as well as a timetable for completing the project.

14. Prepare the design on a word processor, and once you've finished, turn it in to your instructor.

TABLES

Table 11-1: Network Planning and Design Checklist

CHECKLIST FOR NETWORK PLANNING AND DESIGN	
Determine the objectives of the network.	
Inventory user needs and expectations of the network, including network access requirements.	
Inventory legacy components that will be used on the network.	
Extrapolate for future growth.	
Select the access method and cabling infrastructure.	
Determine the fault tolerance requirements.	
Select the Network layer protocol.	
Determine the physical security requirements.	
Select the network operating system.	
Select and source the equipment, including an itemized cost.	
Create a network floorplan, including a cable labeling scheme.	
Determine the need for user training and its extent.	
Submit a budget for approval, and revise it as necessary.	
Prepare an implementation schedule.	
Prepare a schedule for implementation and installation.	

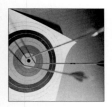

Feedback

LAB QUESTIONS

1. Why is it important to know the client operating system before selecting the server operating system?
2. Why should the LAN described in Figure 11-2 use TCP/IP as the Network layer protocol?
3. What is the advantage of using a hub that supports management?
4. Why is it necessary to know the make, model, and type of peripherals used with a Windows 2000 Server?
5. What are the advantages of thorough network planning before installing a network?

Configuring a Windows Client

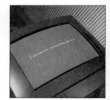

Operating System Technology

OBJECTIVES

1. Select and configure a Windows 2000 Professional client for a Windows 2000 Server domain.
2. Specify client identification parameters.
3. Specify the level of sharing access.

RESOURCES

1. Network+ Certification Training Guide
2. Windows 2000 Professional workstation with a configured network card
3. Network domain name
4. Installed and configured network adapter

DISCUSSION

There are millions of stand-alone computers running Windows 2000 Professional. Many of these will be connecting to a Windows 2000 Server in a network setting. Others will require remote access to the Internet. Windows 2000 Professional is the most versatile operating system available, and comes equipped with out-of-the-box capabilities for connection to either, or both.

Windows 2000 can be used as a client for many different types of server software. You can select from Microsoft or Novell. The drivers for these are pre-installed in Windows 2000 Professional. If your client will be running another operating system, Windows enables you to install it. In this procedure, you will in-stall (if you have not already done so) Microsoft client software.

Client identification is necessary in a network to differentiate between clients. This is done by providing the client with a unique name, specifying their membership is a workgroup, and providing some information about the capabilities of the client computer.

**Operating
System
Technology**

PROCEDURE

1. Log on as **Administrator** at the Login screen.

2. Navigate the *Start/Settings/Control Panel/System* path and click on the **System** icon. (You can also press the **WIN + BREAK** keys at the same time to pop-up the same window.)

3. Select the **Network Identification** tab and then click on the **Properties** button. The *Identification Changes* dialog box opens, as shown in Figure 12-1.

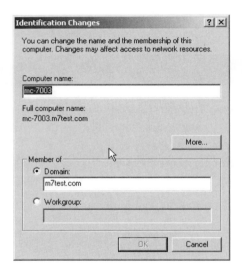

**Figure 12-1: Setting Up
Network Identification**

4. Select a computer name for network identification and enter it into the *Computer name* field.

The computer name is a unique name, consisting of up to 15 alphanumeric characters, identifying the particular client on the network. Windows 2000 will resolve the individual clients to specific IP addresses, and it will use the names of the clients to do so. Because all clients must have unique names for this to occur, record the name of the client in Table 12-1.

5. In the *Member of* frame, click on the **Domain** field.

6. Enter the name of the Domain that the client will log on to after it is connected to the Windows 2000 Server.

For this procedure, you should record all the data for the client workstation in Table 12-1. This will provide you with documentation of the parameters set up for the client. If changes occur at a later date, you will have baseline data information on which to work.

Refer to your network plan (or your instructor) to determine the correct domain name for the client you are working with. Windows 2000 will use this information, as well as other data you'll provide, to secure a client/server relationship between the two nodes. When you are sure of the domain name, enter it into the Domain field and record it in Table 12-1.

7. Click on the **OK** button.

8. Enter the username and password that was provided by your instructor in their corresponding fields and click on the **OK** button.

9. After a few moments, a dialog box should pop up that says *Welcome to the domain.* Click on the **OK** button.

10. Another dialog box will pop up to inform you that you need to reboot for the changes to take effect. Click on the **OK** button.

11. After the computer reboots, log on with your username and password, and make sure that the *Domain* field is set to the domain you just joined. The *Username* and *password* entries are case-sensitive.

You are now connected to the domain and you now have access to all the computers connected to that domain. The server that assigns user rights to your computer decides what items you will be able to access and what you can't. These rights are based on the profile set up at the server for the user attempting to access it.

12. On the desktop, double-click on the **My Network Places** icon.

13. Double-click on the **Entire Network** icon.

14. In the lower left-corner of the page, click on the **Entire Contents** link, as shown in Figure 12-2.

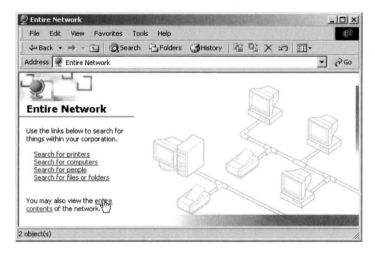

Figure 12-2: The Entire Network

15. Double-click on the **Microsoft Windows Network** icon.

16. Double-click on the name of the domain you joined.

17. You should see the name of the your computer. Double-click on that computer.

If you have any shares on the computer, they should be listed here.

18. Click on the **Back** button and try to access another computer.

You may or may not be able to access other computers, based on your rights. Rights will be examined in a later lab.

TABLES

Table 12-1

CLIENT CONFIGURATION SETTINGS	
Parameter	Value
Domain Name	
Computer Name	

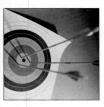

Feedback

LAB QUESTIONS

1. What is the advantage to recording the client information in Table 12-1?
2. What network client software was installed during this Lab?
3. Why was it necessary to enter a computer name on the "Network Identification" page?
4. Why might you not be able to access shares on other people's computers?

Installing Windows 2000 Professional Over a LAN

OBJECTIVES

1. Install the Windows 2000 Professional network client operating system over an existing Local Area Network.

Operating System Technology

RESOURCES

1. Network+ Certification Training Guide
2. Windows 2000 Professional workstation
3. Windows 2000 Server
4. Windows 2000 Professional CD

DISCUSSION

Windows NT had been the Microsoft operating system used for business networking for some time. However, many companies are converting over to the Windows 2000 operating system. When configured correctly, this operating system can be a remarkably powerful tool.

This procedure will guide you through the installation of the Windows 2000 Professional operating system over an existing network. The network installation is very similar to doing a fresh install, but since this install will be an upgrade install instead of a fresh install, all the previous settings will remain configured.

During this installation, you will actually upgrade the previous Windows 2000 Professional installation. The only time you would really be likely to do this is when there are errors in your previous Windows 2000 installation. The main point of doing so in this procedure is that the steps are nearly the same as those you would use if you were upgrading from a Windows 98 or NT workstation.

In a fresh installation, you can configure things such as Regional Settings, File Systems, and which components to install. The default file system is NTFS because it offers better securities. FAT32 is supported if backward compatibility with Windows 9x is needed, because Windows 9x can't read an NTFS file system. This procedure is meant to be performed on an NTFS file system. It will not work correctly with a FAT32 file system.

**Operating
System
Technology**

PROCEDURE

1. Navigate the *Start/Run* path.

2. When the *Run* dialog box appears, type **\\SERVER\2000Pro\i386\winnt32.exe**.

   SERVER stands for the name of the Windows 2000 Server containing the shared folder 2000Pro. This is the path used to begin the installation, as shown in Figure 13-1.

3. Next, click on the **OK** button.

4. After the *Windows 2000 Setup* window appears, click on the **Upgrade to Windows 2000** field, and click on the **Next** button.

Figure 13-1: Installation Running Path

5. Take a few minutes to view the license agreement, scrolling as needed. When you have finished, click on the **I accept this agreement** option, and click on the **Next** button.

6. Enter the Windows 2000 Professional CD Key in the format "xxxxx-xxxxx-xxxxx-xxxxx," and click on the **Next** button.

The progress of the file copying process is displayed, as shown in Figure 13-2. When it is done, the computer will restart automatically.

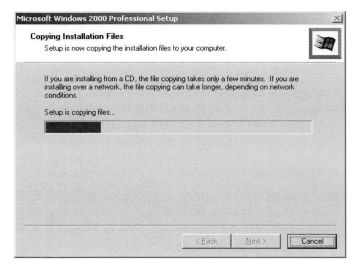

**Figure 13-2:
Installation Progress**

Upon restart, the installation will start up to "Windows 2000 Professional Setup," with white text on a blue background. The Windows 2000 setup wizard will continue to copy files. The computer will automatically restart itself after it has finished copying the files.

7. Wait while Windows is *Installing Devices* and is configuring *Networking Settings*.

8. Next, the wizard will present the *Installing Components* screen.

9. Windows will complete the installation and display the *Performing Final Task* message.

When the installation is completed, the computer will automatically restart itself. When it does, it will load the Windows 2000 Professional operating system. The installation should now be completed.

Feedback

LAB QUESTIONS

1. What is the file system used by Windows 2000 Professional in this lab procedure?
2. What was the first path that was run in order to install Windows 2000 Professional?
3. What file systems will Windows 2000 run on?
4. What are some advantages of the NTFS file system?
5. What are some of the differences between an upgrade install and a fresh install?

Configuring Network User Accounts

OBJECTIVES

1. Install Window 2000 Server tools on a Windows 2000 Professional workstation.
2. Set up a User Account on the Windows 2000 Server.
3. Change the access control parameters for a client workstation so that users are verified in a domain.

Networking

RESOURCES

1. Network+ Certification Training Guide
2. Windows 2000 Professional workstation
3. Windows 2000 Server
4. Network access to Windows 2000 Server tools
5. Shared USERS folder on the Windows 2000 Server

DISCUSSION

In a previous Lab Procedure, you created a network plan, taking into consideration the conditions under which the network would need to operate with Windows 2000 Server software installed. Your instructor has seen to it that the server software has been properly installed according to some of the specifications determined in the network plan. The server has been connected to the clients through the hub. In this lab procedure, you will integrate the server into the existing peer-to-peer LAN to create a server-based LAN. In order to accomplish this goal, you must create a user account on the server for users who will access the network.

Windows 2000 provides for extensive configurations of user accounts. In this procedure, you will set up an account that is relatively simple. In doing so, you will have an opportunity to experiment with the software used for creating client accounts on the server. In a following procedure, you will look at client accounts in more detail by adding additional levels of complexity.

For the server part of this procedure, you will work with the User Manager for Domains, an administrative tool that comes with Windows 2000. With the tool, you can:

- Select a domain, or computer, to administer.
- Create and manage various user accounts.
- Create and manage networked groups.
- Manage the security policies of users and the network.

But first, you need to install the Windows 2000 Server tools. Windows 2000 Server tools are a collection of utilities that make it possible for a user at a client computer, in this case a Windows 2000 Professional client, to remotely manage a Windows 2000 Server computer on a network. Windows 2000 Server tools are also referred to as client-based network administration tools.

The Windows 2000 Server tools that are available for installation on a Windows 2000 Professional client computer are: **Terminal Services Client, Active Directory Domains and Trusts, Active Directory Sites and Services, Active Directory Users and Computers, Certification Authority, Cluster Administrator, Connection Manager Administration Kit, DHCP, Distributed File System, DNS, Internet Authentication Service, Internet Services Manager, QoS Admission Control, Remote Storage, Routing and Remote Access, Telephony,** and **Terminal Services Licensing**. These tools are Windows 2000 Professional versions of the same tools that ship with Windows 2000 Server.

There is no accommodation made for picking or choosing which Windows 2000 Server tools to install, because they are all installed as a single package.

Although in Windows NT 4.0 there were client-based administration tools for Windows 9x, Windows 2000 does not support administration tools for these clients.

Networking

PROCEDURE

1. From a running Windows 2000 Professional client, log on as **Administrator** at the *Login* screen.

2. Type **marcraft** as the password unless otherwise directed by your instructor.

Table 14-1 lists the generic password used in this networking arrangement. If your instructor has provided specific passwords other than the generic ones, use Table 14-1 to record them. The passwords for the Local Administrator and Domain Administrator should be the same.

3. From the desktop, navigate the *Start/Run* path and open the *Run* dialog box.

4. In the *Run* dialog box, type the path **\\SERVER\2000Server\i386\AdminPak.msi**.

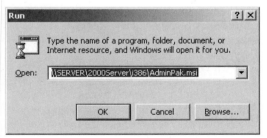

Figure 14-1: Admin Pak Installation Path

SERVER stands for the name of the Windows 2000 Server containing the shared folder *2000Server\i386*. This is the running path used to begin the installation, as shown in Figure 14-1.

5. Click on the **OK** button.

After a moment, the *Windows 2000 Administration Tools Setup Wizard* will start.

6. When the *Welcome to the Windows 2000 Administration Tools Setup Wizard* screen appears, click on the **Next** button.

Administration Tools Installation will begin. A progress bar is available so you can know when it approaches the end of installation.

7. When the install is done, click on the **Finish** button to close the installation program.

Now that you have the Windows 2000 Administration tools installed, you can add your first user.

8. Navigate the *Start/Settings/Control Panel/Administrative Tools/Active Directory Users and Computers* path (installed earlier in this procedure).

The *Active Directory Users and Computers* window, shown in Figure 14-2, will open.

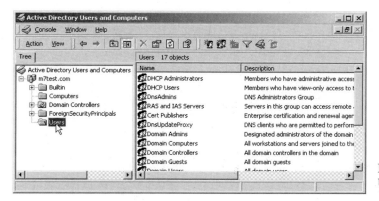

Figure 14-2: Active Directory Users and Computers

9. Right-click on the **Users** folder and select **New/User**.

The *New User* dialog box will open. This is where you will create four user accounts. This includes usernames, fullnames, passwords, access privileges and so forth. For example, the first username and fullname would be your full name without any spaces, followed by the alphanumeric "1" character; the password would be "*getin.*" The second username and fullname would be identical to the first, with the exception that the alphanumeric character "2" would follow the username and fullname. The password for the second user would also be "*getin.*" The third username and fullname would be that of your lab partner, followed by the alphanumeric character "1", with a password of "*getin*". The fourth username and fullname would again be that of your lab partner, followed by the alphanumeric character "2". In Windows 2000, the username and the fullname must be unique for every new account.

10. Observing the statements just given, enter the first user's username and fullname, and click on the **Next** button to continue.

11. Type **getin** for the password, enable the **User cannot change password** option, and click on the **Next** button to continue.

12. Read the summary of the new account and click on the **Finish** button.

13. Repeat steps 9 through 12 for the next three users.

The list of users in *Active Directory Users and Computers* window will now show the users you have just created.

Windows 2000 eases much of the administrative efforts involved in setting up the accounts by supplying a number of default groups that you can use for users who share similar resource needs. You are not bound by the default group lists and may create your own if they do not meet your needs. For this procedure, you are using the defaults and assuming that the accounts you are setting up are for normal users who do not have any specialized needs or circumstances.

14. Right-click on the first username you created and select **Properties** from the pop-up menu.

The *User Properties* dialog box will open, as shown in Figure 14-3.

15. Select the **Member Of** tab at the top of the window.

16. In the *Member Of* window, click on the **Add…** button.

17. The *Select Groups* dialog box, shown in Figure 14-4, will appear. Before configuring the account, we need to clarify some terminology:

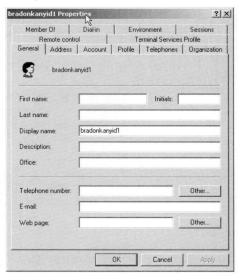

Figure 14-3: User Properties Dialog

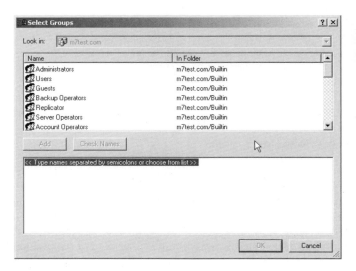

Figure 14-4: Selecting a Group

- A *domain* is a method of organizing shared resources on a network. These include printer shares, file access and storage, CD-ROMs, and other devices. The resources are available to users through controlled access methods determined by network administrators or other users who have been granted permissions and rights for assigning the resources. In order to have access to the network resources in a domain, a user must have an account that includes a username and a password.

- A *user group* is a tool in Windows 2000 that enables you to collect numerous (an unlimited amount of) accounts into a single group with similar attributes and needs for the network resources. Rights and permissions are assigned to a user group, along with mundane items such as the days of the week that a user can access the network.

- A *user account* is an account describing the rights and permissions of an individual user. Typically, user accounts are organized into a single group account, individual user accounts being distinguished by username and password, but all other attributes are the same. A user account may be a member of one or more group accounts. For example, an ordinary user may be a member of the "Domain Users" group, which is for ordinary users. But this user may have some additional training that prepares them for membership in another group, such as the "Domain Admins" group.

- A *local group* is used for assigning rights and permissions for a stand-alone server, or for all servers in a domain. When a local group is created, the rights and permissions described for the group are replicated to all domain controllers, because a domain account appears on all of them.

- A *global group* is a conceptual entity that cannot actually do anything on its own. It is created by organizing user accounts into it, which are, in turn, assigned to group accounts. Think of it as a very flexible organizational tool that enables many different users, having many different levels of rights and permissions, to access similar resources on a domain.

18. Scroll through the built-in list of groups available with Windows 2000 that are shown in Figure 14-4. For most users, the "Domain Users" group includes the attributes that are commonly needed on a LAN. This is shown in the figure as "Domain Users".

19. Click on the **Cancel** button to return to the *User Properties* screen.

20. Select the **Profile** tab.

There are two aspects of a user profile that may be set up at the *Profile* screen, as shown in Figure 14-5.

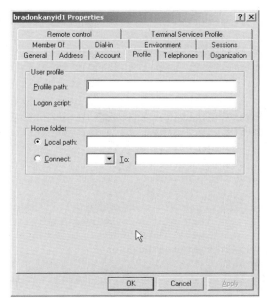

Figure 14-5: Setting User Profile Settings

The first aspect is a login script that automates user logins, and includes any specified drive mapping that is set up for the user; the second is the option of specifying a home directory where user files will be placed. This procedure will concentrate on the second use of the environment profile.

A *home directory* can be created for each network user. All work can be saved in this folder, or subdirectory. The reason for creating a home directory is to centralize the work of all users, making it easier to perform targeted data backups.

In this way, no matter which client a user logs on to the network with, their work will be saved to their individual directory on the server. Alternatively, you can create a home directory on a local client workstation.

21. Select the **Account** tab, and click on the **Logon Hours** button.

The *Logon Hours* dialog box, shown in Figure 14-6, is displayed.

This screen is used to change the times when a user has access to the network. The default is 100% of the time.

We will now disallow the user "yname" from accessing the network on Saturday, and from 1:00 PM until 6:00 PM on Wednesday.

22. Click on the **Saturday** button.

23. Click on the **Logon Denied** field.

24. Highlight from 1:00 AM to 6:00 PM on Wednesday.

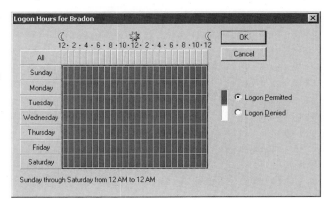

Figure 14-6: Logon Hours Dialog Box

25. Click on the **Logon Denied** field.

26. Click on the **OK** button.

27. Click on the **Logon Hours** button.

28. Now, remove the access restrictions from the account by clicking on the **Saturday** button, and then selecting **Logon Permitted**.

29. Click on the **Wednesday** button, and select **Logon Permitted**.

30. Click on the **OK** button.

Logon hours are useful to ensure that no users can have network access during times of scheduled maintenance.

In the *User Properties* window, at the bottom of the *Account* tab, you will see the option *Account expires*. With this feature, you can establish expiration dates for passwords. The default is for the account to never expire. If you choose an expiration date (the date that an employee's termination becomes effective, for example), the account will expire at the end of that day.

31. Click on the **Log On To** button from *User Properties*.

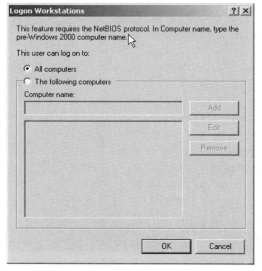

Figure 14-7: Logon Workstations

The *Logon Workstations* dialog box, shown in Figure 14-7, is used to stipulate which workstations, if any, a user can use to log on to the network. The default is to permit logging on from all workstations in the domain.

32. Leave the screen at the default, and click on the **OK** button.

33. Select the **Dial-in** tab in the *User Properties* dialog box.

34. This screen gives users permission to use dial-up networking from a workstation to access the server. Make sure the field *Deny Access* is selected, and click on the **OK** button.

35. Close the *Active Directory Users and Computers* window.

At this point, you have set up four accounts on the server. Now, you must log off and log on as one of these users.

36. Press **CTRL+ALT+DEL** to access the *Windows Security* screen.

37. Click on the **Logoff...** button.

38. Click on the **Yes** button.

39. Login with **YourName1** for the username, type **getin** for the password, and make sure the Domain is set to **Domain**. Click on **OK**.

The *Getting Started with Windows 2000* screen will appear, as shown in Figure 14-8.

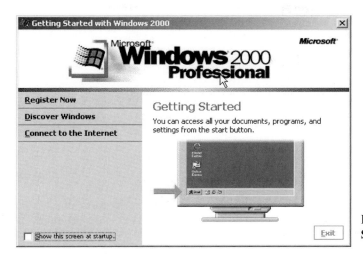

Figure 14-8: Getting Started with Windows 2000

40. Click on the **Exit** button.

Windows 2000 Professional will set up personalized settings. The username and password will be verified on the Windows 2000 Server, and the account you set up will be invoked for the workstation.

In this procedure, you have entered the minimum amount of information needed to create new user accounts from a client machine on a Windows 2000 network. If workstations still need access to one another's directories, you can always set up shares and drive mappings as described in previous Labs. In the next experiment, you will take a more detailed look at client configurations invoked from the Windows 2000 server. As you will discover, the "yname" account still needs some work.

TABLES

Table 14-1: Specific Password Information

PASSWORDS		
Type of Password	**Generic**	**Specific**
Local Administrator	Marcraft	
Domain Administrator	Marcraft	

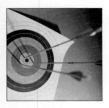

Feedback

LAB QUESTIONS

1. What is the purpose of installing Windows 2000 Server tools on a workstation?

2. How many administrative tools are installed on the client machine after the procedures are completed?

3. If you wanted to block a user from network access on Thursday from 10:00 AM until 12:00 noon, what tool would you use?

4. A user has requested that her home directory be changed from the server to her workstation. Describe how to do so.

5. You receive a request from a Supervisor for logon rights to all four workstations in his department. This is necessary, he explains, so that if an employee is not at work, other employees in the department will be able to access needed files. Describe how to make the change.

6. While you take a well-deserved vacation, you delegate authority for making user account changes to your trusted associate, Igor. What change(s) must you make to Igor's account?

Using Microsoft Management Console

OBJECTIVES

1. Describe the purpose of Microsoft Management Console.
2. Experiment with using snap-ins.
3. Cover some of the common snap-ins.

**Operating
System
Technology**

RESOURCES

1. Network+ Certification Training Guide
2. Windows 2000 Professional workstation in the domain

DISCUSSION

The Microsoft Management Console (MMC) is an extendable common console for managing computers and networks. Using MMC, you can create and modify custom management tools, and access them from either the server or any client.

The MMC does not have any management tools itself. It allows you to add snap-ins to help you with your work. Snap-ins are to MMC what plug-ins are to Internet browsers; each is a specific tool that helps manage a specific aspect of a computer or network. You can combine multiple snap-ins to one MMC to make your own customized management tool.

Many common snap-ins are: **Computer Management**, **Event Viewer**, **Group Policy**, **Local Users and Computers**, and **Active Directory** tools. As you can see, many of these share names with separate Administrative Tools, which are just snap-ins to the MMC. Most of these snap-ins will be used in later chapters.

In this Lab, you will add a few snap-ins to an empty console, and see how to use them.

**Operating
System
Technology**

PROCEDURE

1. Log on as **Administrator** at the *Login* screen.

2. Navigate the *Start/Run* path.

3. Type **MMC.EXE** and click on the **OK** button.

You should see a window similar to Figure 15-1.

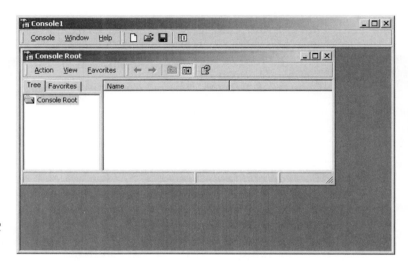

**Figure 15-1: The MMC
Console Window**

4. Navigate the *Console/Add-Remove* snap-in.

5. Click on the **Add** button.

You should see a window similar to Figure 15-2.

**Figure 15-2: The Add
Standalone Snap-in Window**

6. Click on **Computer Management** and click on the **Add** button.

7. Select the **Local Computer** option box and click on the **Finish** button.

8. Click on the **Close** button in the *Add Standalone Snap-in* window.

9. Click on the **OK** button in the *Add/Remove Snap-in* window.

Now the window looks basically the same as if you were to choose the "Computer Management" tool from "Administrative Tools." This is because, as stated earlier, all the administrative tools use MMC as their framework.

10. Navigate through the new options in the window.

Now we are going to add another tool, the Event Viewer.

11. Repeat steps 4–9 and add the Event Viewer.

Both tools are now available in the left-hand part of the window. By using the MMC, you can create your own customized tools for whatever management job you have.

Another great feature of MMC is the ability to remotely manage computers.

12. Repeat steps 4–9, adding Group Policy.

You should see a window similar to Figure 15-3.

Figure 15-3: The Select Group Policy Object Window

13. Click on the **Browse** button.

14. Select **Default Domain Policy** and click on the **OK** button.

15. In the *Select Group Policy Object* window, click on the **Finish** button.

16. Click on the **Close** button.

17. Click on the **OK** button.

Now you can access and modify the Domain Policy remotely from your client computer.

18. Navigate the *Console/Save* path and choose a name to save your file as.

19. Now if you close MMC, you can reopen the same tools all at once by opening the saved file.

Feedback

LAB QUESTIONS

1. What is MMC used for?
2. What must be used with MMC for it to do any work?
3. Can MMC handle only local management?
4. Can MMC be used with only one tool at a time?

Creating Windows 2000 Global Groups

OBJECTIVES

1. Create Global Groups and assign user accounts to the new groups.
2. Assign the global groups to rights on the Windows 2000 network.
3. Verify the rights of the newly created groups.

Networking

RESOURCES

1. Network+ Certification Training Guide
2. Windows 2000 Professional workstation
3. Windows 2000 Server

DISCUSSION

In this lab procedure, you will extend the capabilities of user accounts to include *groups*. A group is a logical concept in the Windows 2000 operating system, which comes preconfigured with groups that have typical *rights* to the network resources. Windows defines a right as being applied system-wide to Windows 2000. Note that a "right" differs from a "permission." A *permission* is directed to a specific object, such as access to a password-protected file.

You will need to return to "Active Directory Users and Computers" in order to create several new user accounts. Once the accounts are created, you will organize them by placing them in various global groups, which you will also create. Because the groups are unique, you need to assign each one with different rights to the network resources.

Once the setup is completed, verify that the actions you have taken are valid by completing a verification sheet for the assigned rights of the new groups.

Once you have completed this lab procedure, retain the new groups and users because you will need them for the next lab procedure.

You will need to be logged in as Administrator to do the following Lab Procedure.

Networking

PROCEDURE

1. Navigate the *Start/ Programs/Administrative Tools/Active Directory Users and Computers* path.

By default, all new users are members of the Domain Users group. However, for this Lab Procedure, you will create two new groups, and then assign the groups to specific rights. While the process, creating a group and then assigning rights, may appear backward it is the correct sequence. A new group is created from the *Active Directory Users and Computers* window.

2. Right-click on the **Users** folder, and navigate the *New/Group* path.

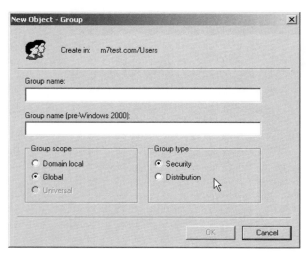

Figure 16-1: Creating a New Group

The *New Object – Group* dialog box will appear, as shown in Figure 16-1.

3. In the *Group name* field, type **YourStationNumber-1**. Example: **Station100-1**.

4. Click on the **OK** button.

You have just added a new global security group. Now you will add some users to the group.

5. Right-click on the group you just created in the *Users* window in the *Active Directory Users and Computers* screen and select **Properties**.

6. Select the **Members** tab in the *Group Properties* dialog box, as shown in Figure 16-2.

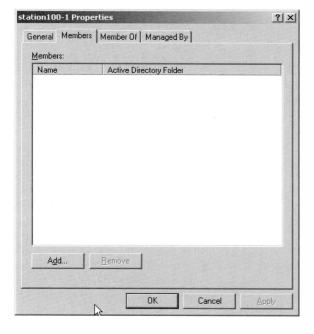

Figure 16-2: Adding Members to a Group

7. Click on the **Add** button.

8. Click on **YourName1**, and click on the **Add** button.

The user "YourName1" will now be listed in the bottom field.

9. Click on **YourPartnersName1**, and click on the **Add** button.

10. Click on the **OK** button.

11. Repeat steps 2–4 to add another Global Group, this time using the name **YourStationNumber-2**.

12. Add **YourName2** and **YourPartnersName2** as members of the group.

At this point, you have set up an account for four new users, created two new groups, and populated each of the new groups with two users each. Now you will look at some of the User Rights available.

13. Close the *Active Directory Users and Computers* window and open **MMC**.

14. Add the **Group Policy** snap-in and add the **Default Domain Controllers Policy**.

The *Group Policy* screen appears.

15. Navigate the *Computer Configuration/Windows Settings/Security Settings/Account Policy* path, as shown in Figure 16-3.

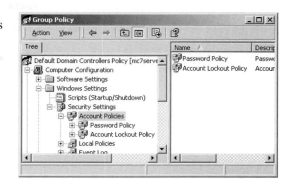

Figure 16-3: The Group Policy

This screen is involved with network passwords and account lockout. Due to the complexity of the screen, take a closer look at the fields:

- Password Policy

  Employees often write down passwords or allow others to use them. Even if they do not, the opportunity for compromising a password increases with time. So, Windows 2000 has a setting that an Administrator can use to establish the **Maximum Password Age** of a password. The default is set for the password to expire in 42 days, but can be set between 1 and 999 days. The user begins receiving notices to change the password 14 days before the expiration date, and if the date is allowed to pass without a change, the user cannot log on until a new password has been selected.

  An option is included for setting the **Minimum Password Age** because many employees become attached to their passwords, and do not like changing them. Often, they will change the password when prompted and then change it back the next day. The minimum age field prevents this from happening.

  The **Minimum Password Length** field is used to ensure a reasonable degree of security by preventing obvious passwords, such as the user's initials. As a good security measure, a password should be, at a minimum, between four and eight characters.

  The **Enforce Password History** field is available so that a user cannot rotate between two or three passwords. The default is to not retain a history of the passwords, but Windows 2000 can remember up to the last 24 passwords that the user has entered.

- Account Lockout Policy

  These fields are used to prevent unauthorized access from someone who randomly enters passwords. The default for the *Account Lockout Threshold* field is 0, which means an important security option is disabled. If you choose to protect the system, set the *Account Lockout Threshold* field at around 5, the maximum. The next field, *Account Lockout Duration*, is used to set the amount of time (in minutes) before you permit another log on attempt.

16. For this Lab Procedure, leave all account policies at their default values.

As mentioned earlier, you must assign groups to a specific right. For example, suppose that you want a group to be able to log on to the server workstation. To do so, you must subscribe the group to that right. Windows 2000 lists specific rights that you may choose from. Now try an example using the two new groups, "YourStationNumber-1" and "YourStationNumber-2".

17. In the *Group Policy* window, navigate the *Computer Configuration/Windows Settings/Security Settings/Local Policies/User Rights Assignment* path.

18. Double-click on **Log On Locally** in the right panel of the window.

19. Closely examine the groups that are permitted to log directly onto the server, and make sure that the "Everyone" group is not listed in the *Assigned To* field of the *Local Security Setting* dialog box.

20. If the "Everyone" group is listed in the *Assigned To* field of the *Local Security Setting* dialog box, uncheck the group in the **Local Policy Setting** field.

21. Click on the **Add** button.

The *Select Users or Groups* dialog box, shown in Figure 16-4, will open. This dialog box is used to assign groups or users to a specific right. In this Lab, you will assign a group to the "Log on locally" right.

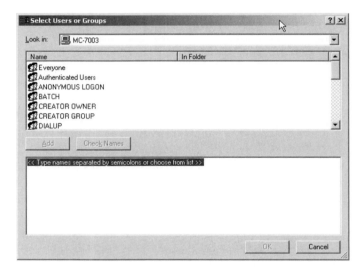

Figure 16-4: Selecting a User or Group

22. Verify that the **Look In** field is set to the domain, not the local computer.

23. Scroll through the listing of names, and highlight your station's first group.

24. Click on the **Add** button.

Your station's first group will appear in the *Add Names* file at the bottom of the box.

25. Click on the **OK** button.

Your station's first group will appear in the *Local Setting* field next to the *Log On Locally* field. This means that the users "YourName1" and "YourPartnersName1" are assigned to the group "YourStation1". You now have the right to log on to the server.

26. Click on the **OK** button in the *Security Policy Setting* dialog box.

27. Assign the right **Access this computer from the network** to the group "YourStation2", making sure that the group "Everyone" is not listed for that right.

28. If the "Everyone" group is listed, highlight it and click on the **Remove** button.

29. Now you can verify the rights assigned to the groups. Table 16-1 contains spaces for you to record the results of confirming the rights.

30. Complete Table 16-1 before continuing.

Without verifying that "Everyone" could log onto the workstation, the group "YourStation1" could not access the server computer through "My Network Places" while the "YourStation2" group could.

31. Give the group "YourStation1" access to the server from the network.

Completing the previous step will help prepare you for an upcoming Lab Procedure.

TABLES

Table 16-1: Group Rights Verification Sheet

GROUP RIGHTS VERIFICATION	
Action	**Results**
Log off the workstation as Administrator. Then, log back on as a member of "YourStation1". Describe the results.	
Double-click on Network Neighborhood, and then double-click on the Server icon. Describe the results.	
Log off and back on again as a member of "YourStation2". Describe the results.	
Double-click on Network Neighborhood, and then double-click on the Server icon. Describe the results.	

Feedback

LAB QUESTIONS

1. Which must you do first, create user accounts, then create a group; or create a group, then create the user accounts? Why?

2. List several configuration settings that can be set up in Account Policy for users and groups.

3. Which is correct? A newly created group may be assigned to a particular right, or a right is assigned to newly created groups.

4. What advantages do groups offer over individual user accounts?

5. Why should Windows 2000 be told to "remember" passwords used in the past?

Sharing Windows 2000 User Directories

OBJECTIVES

1. Describe the share-level permissions available on a Windows 2000 domain.
2. Set up user directories for network sharing.
3. Specify the level of access to user directories, by user account, as well as group account access.
4. From a client computer, verify the access levels set up during the lab procedure.

Operating System Technology

RESOURCES

1. Network+ Certification Training Guide
2. Two Windows 2000 Professional workstations

DISCUSSION

Once a user has an account set up on the network, he/she will require a home directory as a location to save files being worked with. A home directory is nothing more than a folder that is normally created on a server, although it may also be set up on a specific client. Windows 2000 provides for extensive security measures for user directories, and this Lab Procedure will provide you with steps for setting up the permissions, and verifying the level of access.

In the previous Lab Procedure, you configured user accounts for rights, which involved use of network-wide resources. Permissions involve access to specific objects on a network such as files and directories. The share-level permissions that are available to you are:

- *No Access*, disallows any access to the directory or subdirectory and any files contained in it.
- *Read*, allows you to read the contents of a file, subdirectory, or directory, as well as to run application programs stored in the directory.
- *Change*, allows you to modify and create the content of a file, subdirectory, or directory, as well as run application programs.
- *Full Control*, allows you the same create and modify permissions as Change, but also allows you to set permissions to the file, subdirectory, or directory.

Permissions accumulate with group access. For example, if a user has only Read access to a file, but joins a group that has Change access to the same file, then the user will now have Change access. The exception is for No Access, and it overrides all other permissions.

The default for files on a server is to disallow access. Once you set it up for sharing, the level of access is Full Control. This means that any user on the network can access the shared file, subdirectory, or directory. This may be acceptable. Before developing an extensive security plan for hundreds of network users, make sure that it is actually needed.

**Operating
System
Technology**

PROCEDURE

1. Create folders to be shared.

2. Log on as **Administrator** at the *Login* screen.

3. Double-click on the **My Computer** icon.

4. Double-click on an NTFS hard-drive.

5. Navigate the *File/New/Folder* path.

6. Name the folder with **YourName1** using the names you have assigned from the previous Labs.

7. Create three more folders as described in the previous two steps. Name these folders **YourName2**, **PartnersName1**, and **PartnersName2**.

A user has a right to privacy to their files; not for any particular legal reasons, but because the data placed in his/her directory may be confidential. You have numerous options when specifying shares of user files and directories. The ultimate level of privacy is to forbid everyone access, except for the user. However, if you choose this option, only the user can change access permissions. The network administrator will not even be able to access the directory. Most companies have policies describing access permissions, and you should check before blocking out everyone on a network except the user.

8. Share the folders and change the Properties.

9. Highlight the **YourName1** folder and navigate the *File/Sharing* path, as shown in Figure 17-1.

10. Click on the **Share this folder** field.

The window should appear similar to Figure 17-2.

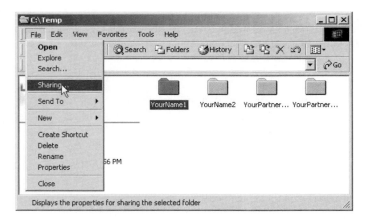

Figure 17-1: Selecting the Sharing Property

11. Click on the **Permissions** button.

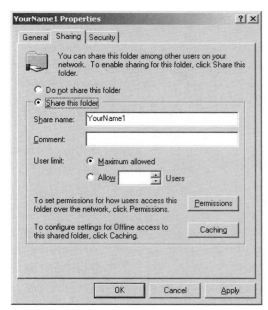

Figure 17-2: Setting Sharing Properties

By default, everyone has Full Control, as in Figure 17-3.

12. Click on the **Everyone** group and click on the **Remove** button.

13. Click on the **Add** button.

You will now see a window similar to Figure 17-4.

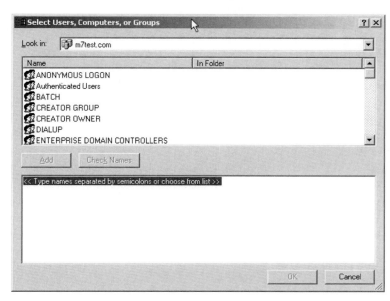

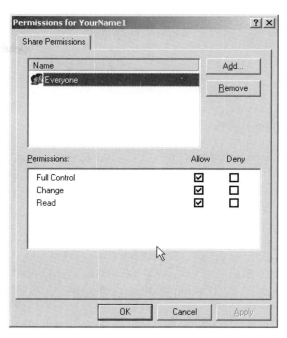

Figure 17-3: Setting Share Permissions

**Figure 17-4: Adding Users
to a Permission**

14. Make sure that the *Look in* field has "domain.com" selected. From the list in the *Names* field, click to highlight **Domain Admins** and click on the **Add** button. "Domain Admins" will now be listed in the lower box.

15. Highlight the **YourStation1** group and click on the **Add** button. This gives the users "YourName1" and "PartnersName1" access to this folder.

16. Click on the **OK** button. The *Share Permissions* list should now have "Domain Admins" and "YourStation1" listed.

17. Click on **YourStation1** and change the *Permissions* field to **Full Access**. Click on the **OK** button.

18. Select the **Security** tab.

19. Uncheck the **Allow inheritable permissions from parent to propagate to this object** field. Click on the **Remove** button if there is a pop-up window, as in Figure 17-5.

20. Verify that the "Everyone" name is highlighted and click on the **Remove** button.

21. Click on the **Add** button.

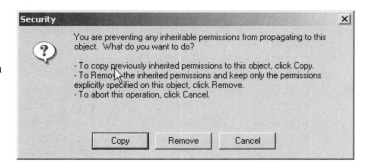

Figure 17-5: Removing Inherited Permissions

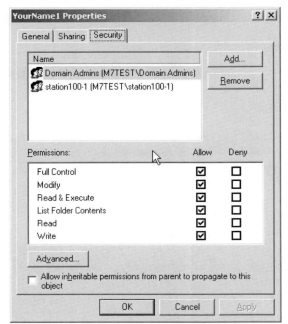

**Figure 17-6:
Security Settings**

22. Highlight **Domain Admins** and click on the **OK** button.

23. Change the *Permissions* field to **Full Access** and click on the **Add** button.

24. Highlight **YourStation1** and click on the **Add** button.

25. Change their permissions to **Full Access**.

The screen should now appear similar to Figure 17-6.

26. Click on the **OK** button on the *Folder Properties* dialog box.

27. Repeat steps 7 through 25 with the remaining folders that you created in steps 5–6, using Figure 17-7 for the access control settings.

28. Create and attempt access to a text file.

SHARE LEVELS FOR SUBDIRECTORIES		
Folder Name	**Access through Share Permissions**	**Directory Permissions**
YourName1	Domain Admins - Read YourStation1 - Full Control	Domain Admins - Full Control YourStation1 - Full Control
YourName2	Domain Admins - Read YourStation2 - Full Control	Domain Admins - Full Control YourName2 - Full Control
PartnersName1	Domain Admins - Read YourStation2 - Read	Domain Admins - Full Control YourStation2 - Read
PartnersName2	Domain Admins - Read PartnersName2 - Full Control	Domain Admins - Full Control PartnersName2 - Full Control

Figure 17-7: TCP/IP Properties Window

29. Double-click on the **YourName1** folder.

30. Navigate the *File/New/Text Document* path.

31. Name the document after the folder in which it resides, "YourName1.txt".

32. Double-click on the file and type **This is a test** into the contents of the file.

33. Navigate the *File/Exit* path. Click on **Yes** to save the changes. Close the *YourName* folder.

34. Repeat steps 28 through 32 with the other three folders, naming the files according to the folder in which they reside.

35. Log off and log in with the usernames indicated in Table 17-1.

36. For each user, attempt the actions described in Table 17-1 and record the results.

37. To simulate a network connection, attempt all access through "My Network Places" and then click on your computer's name (station #), NOT through "My Computer." This will simulate a network connection to your computer.

38. In the *Explanation* column of Table 17-1, describe why you received the result for each attempt.

TABLES

Table 17-1: Subdirectory Share Verification Sheet

ACCESS ATTEMPTS			
User Logon	**Action**	**Result**	**Explanation**
YourName1	Attempt to access and modify YourName1.txt in YourName1. Attempt to access and modify YourName2.txt in YourName2. Attempt to access and modify PartnersName2.txt in PartnersName2.		
YourName2	Attempt to access and modify YourName1.txt in YourName1. Attempt to access and modify YourName2.txt in YourName2. Attempt to access and modify PartnersName1.txt in PartnersName1.		
PartnersName1	Attempt to access and modify YourName1.txt in YourName1. Attempt to access and modify PartnersName1.txt in PartnersName1. Attempt to access and modify PartnersName2.txt in PartnersName2.		
PartnersName2	Attempt to access and modify PartnersName2.txt in PartnersName2. Attempt to access and modify PartnersName1.txt in PartnersName1. Attempt to access and modify YourName2.txt in YourName2.		

Feedback

LAB QUESTIONS

1. What are the four share level permissions available with Windows 2000?

2. A user has "Full Access" to a subdirectory file. The user was prevented from accessing the file when he/she became a member of a group that had access to it. Now, the user has only "Read" access. How do you explain this?

3. In the preceding question, describe how the user can remain a member of the group while retaining "Full Access" to the file.

4. If the right assigned to a user prohibits them from signing on to the server, what will happen once they log on to a client workstation?

5. What is the default share level for directories, subdirectories, and files on an NT server?

Managing User Accounts on NTFS

OBJECTIVES

1. Describe permissions available for NTFS.
2. Set user and groups permissions located on NTFS.
3. Describe conventions used with NTFS permissions.
4. Verify permissions set up on user accounts.

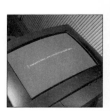

**Operating
System
Technology**

RESOURCES

1. Network+ Certification Training Guide
2. Windows 2000 Professional workstation
3. Windows 2000 Server

DISCUSSION

In the previous Lab Procedure you set up share-level permissions on directories and files. With one exception, the procedure you used to set up permissions is identical to the steps you would take when setting permissions on a FAT partition. But because the subdirectories you worked with were on an NTFS partition, you had to click on the *Security* tab in the *Share Properties* window and include the same permissions.

Why? NTFS allows a greater degree of security than a FAT file structure, which is why Microsoft recommends that you not include a FAT partition on the server hard disk. You are allowed to set permissions only to the directory level on a FAT partition. With an NTFS partition, you can set permissions for the directory, subdirectory, and file levels. In addition, you have more security options to choose from.

In this procedure, you will use the four user accounts from the previous Lab — YourName1, YourName2, PartnersName1, and PartnersName2 — to explore the enhanced security options of NTFS.

PROCEDURE

1. Log on as **Administrator** at the *Login* screen.

2. Open *Windows Explorer*.

**Operating
System
Technology**

3. Select **drive C**.

4. Navigate the *File/New/Folder* path.

5. Click in the *new folder's* name box, type your **firstname** and **lastname**, then press the **ENTER** key.

6. Double-click on your new folder and navigate the *File/New/Text Document* path.

7. Type your partners' **firstname** and **lastname** with **.txt** as the extension, then press the **ENTER** key.

8. Double-click on the icon for the .txt file you just created.

9. When the *Notepad* (or other word processor) screen appears, type **This is a test**.

10. Save the file and close *Notepad*.

11. Navigate to the folder you created in step 5.

12. Right-click on the folder and choose **Sharing**.

13. Click on the **Share This Folder** field, and then click on the **Permissions** button.

14. Remove **Everyone**.

15. Click on the **Add** button and click on **Show Users**.

16. Add **Domain Admins** and **YourName1**, giving them Full Access.

17. Exit from the **Permissions** dialog box.

18. Select the **Security** tab.

19. Click on the **Advanced** button.

20. In the *Access Control Settings* dialog box, select the **Owner** tab.

You should see something similar to Figure 18-1.

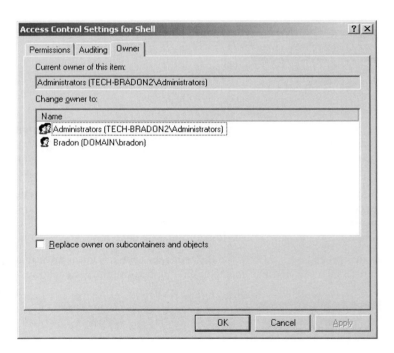

Figure 18-1: Access Control Settings

Notice that the owner of the directory is the Administrator. The reason is because the "firstlast" folder was created when you were logged on as the Administrator. There are many good reasons to leave ownership and Full Access permissions with the Administrator, sharing them with the actual owner. From the user's perspective, none of these reasons are particularly relevant, and this is understandable.

Windows 2000 recognizes that the owner of a file, or directory, has full control over it, and ownership belongs with the actual owner, not the Administrator. For example, you may be the salary administrator in the Human Resource department and maintain salary information in your directory. No matter how much the networking department would like to have a peak at everyone's salary, it is simply none of their business. You, then, should own the directory and decide who has permission to view its contents.

See how this is done by first wresting ownership from the Administrator, and placing it into your hands.

21. Click on the **OK** button to close the *Access Control Settings* window.

22. Click on the **OK** button to close the *Properties* window.

23. Log off as **Administrator** and then log back on as **yourname1**.

24. Open *Windows Explorer*.

25. Navigate to the folder you created in step 5.

26. Right-click on the *yourname1* folder and choose **Properties**.

27. Select the **Security** tab.

28. Click on the **Advanced** button.

29. Select the **Owner** tab.

30. Check the *Replace owner on subcontainers and objects* field.

31. Click on your name in the *Change owner to:* field, then click on the **OK** button.

32. Remove **Administrator** and **Everyone** from the permissions.

33. Click on the **OK** button to close *Folder Properties*.

34. Log off the system, then log on as **Administrator**.

35. Navigate to the folder you created at the beginning of this procedure.

36. Right-click on the *yourname1* folder and choose **Properties**.

37. Select the **Security** tab.

38. Click on the **Permissions** button.

You will receive a message saying you do not have authority to change permissions on the directory; the Administrator no longer has Full Control of your directory. As long as you are logged onto the network, he can change permissions. But what happens if a crisis occurs and access is required to your files when he's not around to let anyone in? For example, suppose he leaves the company without notice and does not bother changing permissions to his directory? Windows 2000 anticipated this, and provided the Administrator with a backdoor key.

39. Click on the **OK** button to close the *Security* window.

40. While logged on as the Administrator, click on the **Advanced** button under the *Security* tab and select the **Owner** tab.

41. Click on **Administrator** in the *Change owner to:* field, and select the **Replace owner on subcontainers and objects** field.

42. Click on the **OK** button to take ownership of the files.

Depending on the original permissions assigned to the directory, you may receive additional prompts describing permissions. In all cases, choose the response that gives the Administrator Full Control of the directory; all others who were given access will be removed. While this may be unfortunate to users or groups that you are not aware of, it is better than losing the information in the directory.

When setting permissions on an NTFS directory or file, you have more security options than when setting permissions on a FAT directory or file.

43. Select the **Security** tab.

The *Permissions* window, shown in Figure 18-2, will open.

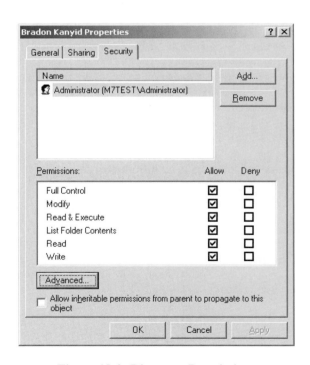

Figure 18-2: Directory Permissions

Some of the permissions shown in the new window are identical to those described in the previous Lab Procedure. To be thorough, these are described below, along with features that were not previously discussed.

- *Read* – enables you to read the contents of a file, subdirectory, or directory. You cannot run application programs stored there, change the files, or add (save) a file to the directory. You may delete a folder with read permissions if there are no files in it.

- *Write* – enables you to add files and subdirectories to the directory and change their attributes. However, it does not grant access to files unless granted by other directory or file permissions. In other words, you are permitted to save a file to the directory but you are not permitted to read it after it has been saved.

- *List Folder Contents* – enables you to browse the files in a folder without being able to access the files for read or write purposes. You can read the attributes and permissions, but not modify them.

- *Read & Execute* – enables all the Read and List Folder Contents permissions, and also enables you to run executable programs in that folder.

- *Modify* – enables you to modify/create the contents of a file, subdirectory, or directory, and run application programs. You can view file/subdirectory names, switch to subdirectories, read data in files, and run application files. You may delete the directory and its files.

- *Full Control* – allows you the same create and modify permissions as the Modify permission, but also allows you to set permissions to and delete the file, subdirectory, or directory. You may also take ownership of the directory as long as you have this right.

44. Click on the **Cancel** button.

Now use some of these permissions on the four users "YourName1", "YourName2", "PartnersName1", and "PartnersName2". Figure 18-3 contains a list of permissions to use on each of the users, and the testfat.txt file contained in their home directories.

SUBDIRECTORY SHARE LEVELs		
Subdirectory Name	**Access Permissions**	**Security Permissions**
YourName1	Administrator/Full Control YourName1/Full Control YourName2/Read	Administrator/Full Control YourName1/Full Control YourName2/Read
YourName2	Administrator/Full Control YourName2/Full Control YourName1/Read	Administrator/Full Control YourName2/Full Control YourName1/Read & Execute
PartnersName1	Administrator/Full Control PartnersName1/Write PartnersName2/Read	Administrator/Full Control PartnersName1/Modify PartnersName2/List Contents
PartnersName2	Administrator/Full Control PartnersName2/Full Control PartnersName1/Read	Administrator/Full Control PartnersName2/Full Control PartnersName1/Read, Write

Figure 18-3: TCP/IP Properties Window

45. After you have set up the permissions, log on as each user and verify the permissions.

46. Complete Table 18-1 by recording the results of each attempt, and briefly explain the result.

TABLES

Table 18-1: Share Verifications for the Subdirectories

SUBDIRECTORY SHARE VERIFICATION			
User Logon	**Action**	**Result**	**Explanation**
YourName1	Attempt to access and modify YourName2.txt in YourName2 directory. Create a text file, and save to YourName2 directory as trial.txt.		
YourName2	Attempt to access and modify YourName1.txt in YourName1 directory.		
PartnersName1	Attempt to access and modify PartnersName1.txt in PartnersName1 directory. Attempt to access and modify PartnersName2.txt in PartnersName2 directory. Create a text file and save to PartnersName2 directory as trial.txt.		
PartnersName2	Attempt to access and modify PartnersName1.txt in PartnersName1 directory.		

Feedback

LAB QUESTIONS

1. How do permissions differ between FAT and NTFS file structures?
2. What can NTFS permissions be applied to? How does this differ from FAT?
3. A person with the Modify permission is allowed to _____.
4. The user "bwill" is a member of the group "Sales." Also, "bwill" has List Folder Contents access to a directory, while "Sales" has Change access to the same directory. What are "bwill's" permissions for the directory?
5. Who should have Full Control permission of a directory? Who should not?

Auditing Files and Directories

OBJECTIVES

1. Establish an audit policy for a computer in a Windows 2000 domain.
2. Set up a directory audit on a Windows 2000 client.
3. View the results of the audit.

**Operating
System
Technology**

RESOURCES

1. Network+ Certification Training Guide
2. Two Windows 2000 Professional workstations
3. Windows 2000 Domain Server with user accounts set up

DISCUSSION

In this Lab Procedure, you will set up an audit on a directory, and its contents. Windows 2000 comes with a couple of tools that are used to monitor usage of files on a network. The auditing function, located in the advanced options of the *Security* tab of a directory or file's *Properties* page, provides information targeted to a particular resource. To see how Windows delivers the results of the audit, you will then make various changes to the directory. After making changes, you will review the results in an Administrative Tool called "Event Viewer."

Auditing is only one of the monitoring tools available; typically, monitoring means troubleshooting. Windows 2000 has a plethora of troubleshooting tools used to identify system and network problems. This Lab Procedure, however, focuses on user accounts and the level of activity associated with the user's files and directories.

An audit may be used to increase the efficiencies of user access to the server resources rather than as a source of troubleshooting data.

PROCEDURE

1. Log on as **Administrator** at the *Login* screen, and open **MMC**.

2. Add the **Group Policy** snap-in, and set the object to **Default Domain Controllers Policy**, as shown in Figure 19-1.

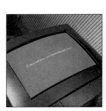

**Operating
System
Technology**

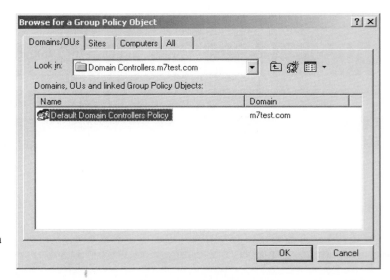

Figure 19-1: Selecting a Group Policy

3. Navigate the *Default Domain Controllers Policy/Computer Configuration/Windows Settings/Security Settings/Local Policies/Audit Policy* path.

Windows 2000 provides several attributes that you can monitor, which can be set to audit on success, fail, or both. Figure 19-2 lists each of them, and includes a short description of the audit. Some thought should be given when auditing in a practical situation. Since the storage files for audits are set by default to a size of 512 kB, the file can fill quickly.

Figure 19-2: Audited Policy Events

POLICY EVENTS TO AUDIT	
Event	**Happens When**
Audit Account Log on Events	A domain controller receives a request to validate a user account.
Audit Account Management	An administrator creates, changes, or deletes a user account or a group. You can also audit such tasks as the renaming, enabling, or disabling of user accounts, as well as changes made to users' passwords.
Audit Directory Service Access	A user gains access to an Active Directory object. To audit this type of event, you must configure the specific Active Directory object.
Audit Log on Events	A user logs on or off, or makes or cancels a network connection.
Audit Object Access	A user gains access to a file, folder, or printer. To audit this type of event, you must configure the specific object to be audited.
Audit Policy Change	A change has been made to the user's security options, rights, or audit policies.
Audit Privilege Use	A user has exercised a privileged right, such as changing the system time.
Audit Process Tracking	A program or procedure has performed an action. This information is most useful to programmers who are tracking the details of program execution.
Audit System Events	A user restarts or shuts down his computer; or an event has occurred that affected the security of the operating system.

4. For this procedure, select all categories, in both the success and failure columns, and click on **OK**.

At this point, you have established the audit policy for the domain. Now, you will specify an object to be audited (a directory) and all the files it contains.

5. Close **MMC** and double-click on **My Computer**.

6. Double-click drive C.

7. Highlight the **YourName2** folder.

8. Navigate the *File/Properties/Security* path.

9. Click on the **Advanced** button.

10. Select the **Auditing** tab.

You should see a window similar to Figure 19-3.

11. Click on the **Add** button.

12. Add the **Everyone** group.

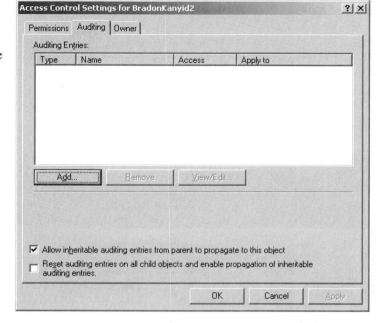

Figure 19-3: Directory Auditing Dialog Box

Now you will see a list of checkboxes for different options. These are the events to audit, and are used to select specific categories that you want to audit.

Near the top of the dialog box is a combo-box that enables you to pick what the audit applies to. The options are:

- This folder only
- This folder, subfolders, and files
- This folder and subfolders
- This folder and files
- Subfolder and files only
- Subfolders only
- Files only

The default is to have the folder, subdirectory, and files audited.

The selection process is essentially a filter enabling the Administrator to monitor usage to a particular resource. While this procedure monitors everyone, this would be too broad an audit in a practical network. Instead, you may want to consider a database that is used heavily by network users: You may audit its usage as a result of receiving complaints that it has become slow in returning files. It is often difficult to determine which users are heavy hitters; an audit will confirm specific users, or groups, that require extended use to the database. Once you know who needs more than occasional access, you can take steps to replicate the database to another machine, and shift those users to that machine.

13. Select all the Events to **Audit**, both **Success** and **Failures**, and click on the **OK** button.

14. Select the **Permissions** tab, add **Everyone** with **Full Control** access, and click on the **OK** button.

15. Select the **Sharing** tab, and add **Everyone** with **Full Control** access.

16. Log out, and log on as **PartnersName1** at the *Login* screen.

17. Open the **YourName2.txt** file in the *YourName2* folder, and type a sentence about conducting file and directory audits as part of this procedure.

18. After making the changes to YourName2.txt, save the file.

19. Now log out, and log on as **YourName1** at the *Login* screen.

20. Open the **YourName2.txt** file, and type a sentence about adding text to the file from a different client machine than the one that was used to type the previous text.

21. Save the newly edited file in its folder, and log out and log on as **Administrator** at the *Login* screen to see the results of the audit.

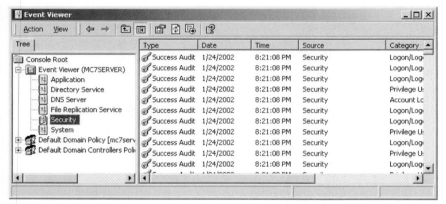

Figure 19-4: Event Viewer Window

22. Navigate the *Start Button/Programs/Administrative Tools/Event Viewer/Console Root/Event Viewer/Security* path.

The *Event Viewer* window appears, similar to that shown in Figure 19-4.

The *Event Viewer* window displays summary information about the network and system, and is often used as a troubleshooting tool. For auditing purposes, it will provide information about the targeted audit under the *Security* option.

23. To view details about an event, double-click on one of the line items that you think is editing the file.

Now you will see some information that can be somewhat cryptic. This is because some of it has no value to anyone except Administrators. In addition, some of the information provided is there only for support assistance from Microsoft, such as the Event ID number, for example.

24. At this time, take a few minutes to browse the details of some of the other events.

Feedback

LAB QUESTIONS

1. List the steps required to set up an audit policy.
2. Where do you review the results of an audit?
3. Who can be the focus of an audit?
4. How can an audit be restricted to a single directory and not include files within the directory?
5. Can an audit be conducted on different directories at the same time?

Installing and Configuring a Network Printer

OBJECTIVES

1. Use Windows 2000 printer installation software to install a printer on the workstation.
2. Use Windows 2000 printer configuration software to set up share parameters for the printer.
3. Install the printer software on a client computer running Windows 2000 Professional.
4. Verify operation of the network printer by sending a print job to the network printer from eligible clients.

Networking

RESOURCES

1. Network+ Certification Training Guide
2. Two Windows 2000 Professional workstations
3. Printer with bi-directional parallel cable connected to the workstation
4. Printer software, if printer drivers aren't preloaded in the computers, or a disk containing the most recent version of the driver software

DISCUSSION

Installing a printer on a server-based LAN consists of three basic tasks:

- *Install the printer on the workstation.* This includes selecting the printer manufacturer and installing drivers that have been preloaded by Windows, or from a disk.

- *Configure the workstation-connected printer as a shared device, and establish the conditions of the share.* This includes parameters such as the time that the printer is available, the users or groups that have access, the method of spooling, and so forth.

- *Install the printer software on the client computers.* This can be done across the network, or at each machine. In this Lab Procedure, you will be accomplishing this at each computer. Once the software is installed, Windows will connect to the printer.

Printer problems are a common source of aggravation on a network because of a basic lack of understanding about the server options. For this reason, the printer setup and configuration screens used with Windows 2000 are described in detail in this Lab Procedure.

The client user can also make changes that will affect that client machine's ability to print. Although the printer is controlled and managed at the server, a misinformed user can easily cripple printing from at least one client. The only safeguard against this is to make sure you document the client's settings in case the user decides to experiment.

In this procedure, you will install and configure a printer at the workstation, then install the same software at another client. The test for a successful printer install is, of course, whether all of the clients can print.

Networking

PROCEDURE

1. Uninstall any printer software on the workstation.

2. Log on as **Administrator** at the *Login* screen.

3. Navigate the *Start/Settings/Printers* path.

When there are not any printers installed, the only icon available will be the *Add Printer* icon.

4. Double-click on the **Add Printer** icon to start the *Printer Wizard*.

The *Add Printer Wizard*, shown in Figure 20-1, will open.

5. Click on the **Next** button.

You now have two options: install a printer to the computer you are working from, or install a networked printer for remote printing.

For this procedure, and in most practical situations, choose the first option—install it to the computer you are now using.

In this procedure, this computer will be the print server. All clients will connect to the server for printing.

6. Uncheck the **Automatically detect and install my Plug and Play printer** checkbox.

7. Click on the **Next** button.

Figure 20-1: Add Printer Wizard

8. When the screen shown in Figure 20-2 appears, select a printer port.

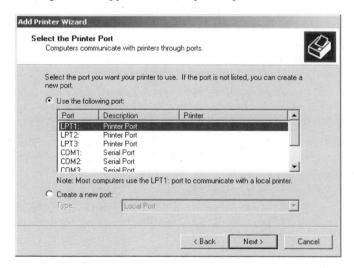

Figure 20-2: Select a Printer Port

9. Choose **LPT1**, unless directed otherwise by your instructor.

10. Click on the **Next** button after selecting a port.

11. At the next screen, choose the manufacturer of your printer.

12. Specify the type of printer in order to install the correct drivers for it.

13. If your printer is not listed either by manufacturer or by specific type, click on the **Have Disk** button.

It is a good idea to install from the disk that came with the printer, if the printer's software is relatively new. It may have drivers that are more current than those pre-installed with Windows.

14. Click on the **Next** button once again.

15. If you are asked to keep or replace the existing driver, choose **Replace** and click on the **Next** button.

A screen similar to that shown in Figure 20-3 appears, asking for a printer name.

If there are older operating systems on a network, they will not support log file names. In such cases, use the 8.3 convention for naming files. It is a good idea to keep the printer's network name short; a long name is a good opportunity for data entry mistakes.

16. After naming the printer, click on the **Next** button.

17. In the next screen, shown in Figure 20-4, click on the **Share as** option, and enter a share name.

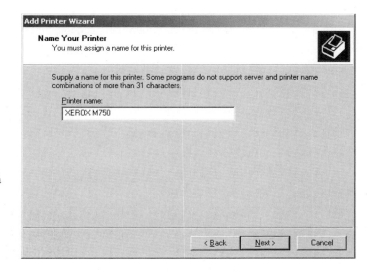

Figure 20-3: Enter a Printer Name

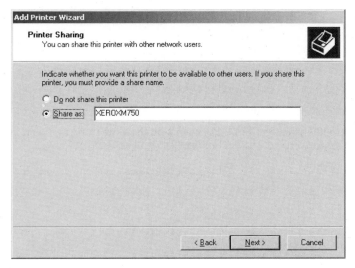

Figure 20-4: Sharing the Printer

18. Click on the **Next** button.

19. In the next screen, enter a location description and comment, and then click on the **Next** button.

20. When asked if you want to print a test page, select the **Yes** option and click on the **Next** button.

21. The next screen shows a summary of all the settings you just set up. Click on the **Finish** button.

22. After the drivers have been installed, try to print a test page.

23. Verify that the test page printed, and click on the **OK** button.

24. Go to *Notepad* and print a simple message.

Up to this point, you have done nothing more than install a printer to the computer. As far as printing is concerned at this stage, it should print like any other stand-alone computer. If the *Notepad* file will not print, let your instructor know what is occurring before going any further.

Assuming that you are able to print from the server machine, you can now configure the printer software you have just installed.

25. Navigate the *Start/Settings/Printers* path.

The *Printers* dialog box will open.

26. Right-click on the **printer** icon (the one just installed) and choose **Properties**.

The *Printer Properties* dialog box is depicted in Figure 20-5.

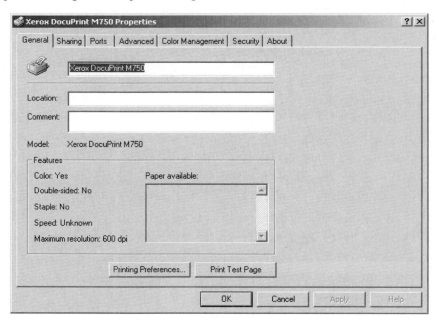

Figure 20-5: Printer Properties Dialog

Under the *General* tab are the following options:
- *Comment* can be used to enter a brief message about the printer.
- *Location* is used to indicate where the printer is. For a network with multiple printers, it can be confusing for users to know where to go to get the document they printed.

Also, there are buttons for *Printing Preferences* and *Print Test Page*.

27. In the *Comment* field, enter your name.

28. In the *Location* field, enter your name.

29. Click on the **Ports** tab.

30. Under the *Ports* tab, you can change the port that the printer prints to.

31. If available, check **Enable bi-directional support** near the bottom of the window.

32. Click on the **Advanced** tab.

In the *Advanced* tab, there are options for scheduling. With these options, you can specify when the printer is available, the priority of print jobs, and how the jobs are to be handled at the printer. The default availability is "Always". If the printer needs to be taken down for scheduled maintenance, you can change this by clicking the *Available from* button, and specifying the time that it will be available.

Review the following settings, and make any necessary adjustments.

- The *Priority* field is used to set the priority level assigned to a printer. This is useful when there are multiple printers on the network. To give a printer priority over another, make the priority number larger.

- *Spool* enables print jobs to be written to a temporary file. When chosen, click "Start Printing immediately" to provide better performance.

- *Print directly to the printer* is more appropriate for a stand-alone computer. If used in a network, print jobs will invariably become mixed. Therefore, it is best to leave it unchecked.

Leave the other checkboxes alone. "Keep printed documents" will save all print jobs to a file. Unless you have a good reason for retaining all users' print jobs, leave it unchecked.

33. Select the **Security** tab.

The *Permissions* dialog box is duplicated in Figure 20-6. Setting permissions for printer access is similar to setting permissions for access to the network. By default, the following permissions have been set up:

- Administrators: full control (i.e., Print, Manage Printers, and Manage Documents)

- Creator Owner: Manage Documents

- Everyone: Print

- Power Users: full control

Review the following settings and make any necessary adjustments.

- *Print* enables a user or group to print documents, but not to change print settings. Use this permission for ordinary network users.

- *Manage Printers* enables the user or group to print, manage documents sent to the printer, and to make configuration changes.

- *Manage Documents* enables a user or group to print, as well as manage the printer. However, configurations settings cannot be changed.

34. Click on the **Add** button, and the *Select Users, Computers, or Groups* dialog box will open.

35. Add the two user groups that you have created in previous Labs to the list with full control access.

36. Click on the **OK** button.

37. Click on the **Advanced** button.

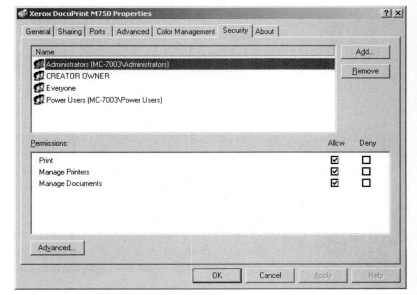

**Figure 20-6:
The Permissions
Dialog Box**

Available in these tabs are "Ownership" and "Auditing". Selecting *Ownership* will reveal the owner of the printer, and allow the Administrator to take control of it. *Auditing* is used to track usage of the printer, and should be used selectively since audit log files are relatively small and will overfill, slowing performance.

38. Click on the **OK** button.

The setup and configuration of the printer is now complete. The clients now need to be made aware that a printer is connected to the network and has been set up as a share device.

39. At another Windows 2000 client machine, double-click **My Network Places**.

40. Locate the computer with the shared printer and double-click the **printer** icon.

You will receive a message similar to the one shown in Figure 20-7.

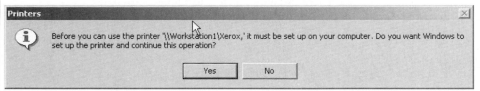

41. Click **Yes** to set up the printer.

You will now see a window similar to Figure 20-8.

42. Navigate the *Printer/ Properties* path.

Figure 20-7: Set Up Printer Confirmation

43. Click on **Print Test Page**.

44. When prompted, choose **test page printed correctly**.

45. Close all windows.

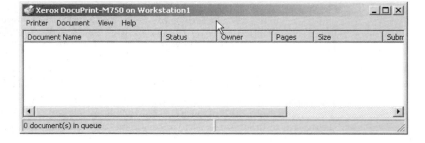

Figure 20-8: Printing a Test Page

LAB QUESTIONS

1. What are your options if, during a network printer install, the type of printer you are installing is not listed in the Windows installation steps?

2. After the printer software is installed on a client, an error message, saying that Windows cannot find the path to the printer, is generated when you attempt a test print. What is the next step?

3. Three printers have their priority slide switches set to Low, Low, and High. Which printer will print first if all three are sent a print job at the same time?

4. Are permissions for access to the printer set up according to the name of the client computer that will be printing to the printer, or according to user and group names?

5. What is the purpose of setting up a separator page?

Feedback

Monitoring Windows 2000 Performance

OBJECTIVES

1. State several uses of monitoring Windows 2000 Performance.
2. Set up and configure an object and counter, and display them in a real-time chart.
3. Set up and configure an object and counter to set an alert threshold.
4. Set up and configure an object and counter for logging.
5. Convert a logged file for display in chart format.

**Operating
System
Technology**

RESOURCES

1. Network+ Certification Lab Guide
2. Windows 2000 Professional workstation
3. Network connection to Windows 2000 Server

DISCUSSION

Windows products, from 3.1 Workgroups to Windows Me, have included some type of performance monitoring software, and Windows 2000 is no different. Using the Windows 2000 Performance tool, you can gauge the effectiveness of a machine's processor, memory, and disk utilization. The significant difference between Windows 2000's Performance tool and versions included with prior versions of Windows is the ability to monitor resources on remote machines.

With the Performance tool, you have the following capabilities:

- The ability to monitor the statistical data on any computer on a network.
- The ability to dynamically change the data that the Performance monitor is gathering.
- The ability to export any of the data to common applications such as a word processor or spreadsheet software.
- The ability to set thresholds for processes that, if exceeded, will generate alerts.
- The ability to execute a program whenever a counter threshold is exceeded.
- The ability to create long-term logs that monitor parameters on different computers.
- The ability to generate reports that compare the recorded activity of a logged parameter to the current activity.

Any device running under Windows 2000 can be monitored using the Performance tool. The parameter that is being monitored is logged in chart form, normally as a line graph or a histogram (which resembles a bar graph).

A network administrator should evaluate the network performance occasionally, so that one node does not dominate the server resources or cause problems across the network by transmitting garbled data. Servers particularly lend themselves to the benefits of performance monitoring because if a bottleneck is suspected in a network, they may be a source of the problem. The time required for a processor to execute tasks, or the time required for the hard drive to access a file, can grow as users are added to a LAN. Therefore, a periodic analysis of these components should be conducted to ensure that the server's capabilities are keeping pace with the needs and demands of the users.

If, however, the server appears to be holding up its responsibilities, the Performance tool can also be used to evaluate the speed at which the network can be accessed. Again, over time, and as more users are added, access to the technology will slow.

In this procedure, you will examine several objects and counters associated with Windows 2000. An **object** is a network resource, either physical (e.g., a microprocessor) or logical (e.g., a software command). Objects are controlled by managed systems, which, in turn, contain groups of similar objects. The Performance tool is a managed system. The system, then, is organized into a group of similar systems related by counters. A **counter** specifies the attribute of an object, describing the statistical data (the absolute value of an object) that the Performance tool will collect on a chosen object. The Performance tool also enables you to determine the instance of a data collection session. An instance refers to how many of the same objects are being monitored during the session. For example, a server may have two or more processors, and an instance refers to each of the processors.

Each object listed in the Windows 2000 performance system contains several counters. For example, one of the counters for the processor object is *& Processor Time* (the time that the processor is in use). The counter "counts" the seconds that the processor is active, and displays the count as a percentage of the total time. In other words, all of the Windows 2000 objects in the Performance tool generate statistical data describing the operation of the network resources.

As with any data collection system, you must review and summarize the statistical data, make a determination of the root-cause of a problem, and then take corrective actions to fix the problem. The Performance tool helps you identify the root-cause of problems. When combined with an intimate understanding of networking, it is a very valuable tool. Let us see how it works.

Operating System Technology

PROCEDURE

1. Log on as **Administrator** at the Login screen.

2. Navigate the *Start/Programs/ Administrative Tools/Performance* path.

The *Performance* window, shown in Figure 21-1, will open. If no objects have been selected to run, the window will be blank.

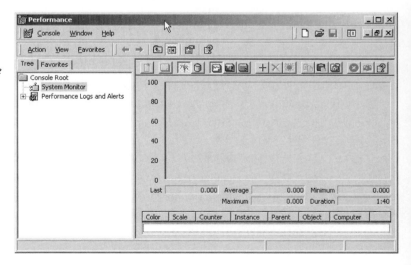

Figure 21-1: Performance Tool

You may notice that there is no menu interface for the Performance monitor. All the options are available through the button toolbar above the monitor.

3. To monitor the *% Processor Time*, click on the **Add** button.

The *Add Counters* dialog box, shown in Figure 21-2, will open.

The options available are:

- *Computer*: This is the computer, either local or networked, that you want to monitor.
- *Performance object*: This is the object that you want to monitor. Some examples would be: Processor, Server, TCP, Memory, and DNS.
- *Counter*: These are different things you can monitor that are within the selected Performance Object.
- *Instance*: Some objects may have several instances, such as multiple processors. You can select all instances, or select an instance from a list.

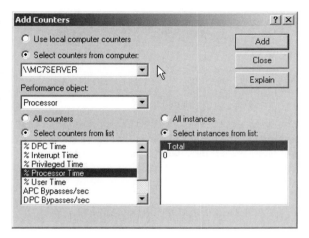

4. Add a counter with the following options:

Figure 21-2: Add Counters

- Computer: Type in the name of the server. If you do not know the name, ask your instructor.
- *Performance Object*: **Processor**
- *Counter*: **% Processor Time**
- *Instance*: **_Total**

Then click on the **Close** button.

This will return you to the *Performance* window, and the *% Processor Time* counter will be added to the chart, where it will start logging data.

You should now be viewing the processor time of the remote computer from your own computer. This feature is not typically available to all users, simply because not everyone needs to know what their co-workers are doing. But the network administrator needs to know this so that usage matches the capabilities of each machine, as well as the bandwidth of the network. In addition, the administrator can query the server from a remote location to make sure it is performing correctly.

You can also change options for the graphing, such as color, thickness, scale, and style.

5. Right-click on the counter in the bottom section of the screen and choose **Properties**.

The *System Monitor Properties* dialog box will now appear.

6. Click on the **Data** tab.

Now the *Data* dialog box will be shown, as shown in Figure 21-3.

Near the bottom of the dialog box are different drop-down menu options that affect characteristics of how the counter is graphed.

7. Click on the **OK** button to close the dialog box.

8. Let the monitor run for a few minutes to collect data.

Windows 2000 enables you to chart more than one parameter at a time. This is why the attributes of the chart lines (color, width, scale) are listed as options in the *Data* dialog box. Now another counter will be added to the Performance monitor.

9. Return to the *Add Counters* dialog box, and add the **Interrupts/sec** counter to the chart using the same processor object.

10. Change the line color of the new counter to **Red**.

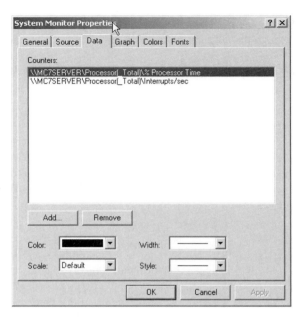

Figure 21-3: The Data Dialog Box

Figure 21-4 shows an example of these counters running, as the Performance tool charts them.

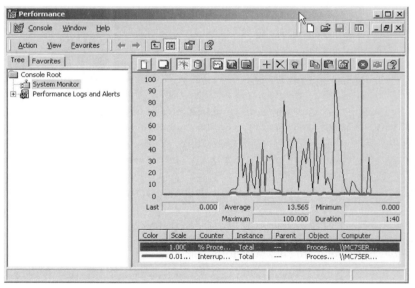

Figure 21-4: The Running Counters

11. Click on the **New Counter Set** button.

The chart currently running will be cleared.

12. Click on the **Add Counter** button, and add the following counter:

> *Computer*: **Local computer**
>
> *Object*: **Server**
>
> *Counter*: **Bytes Transmitted/sec**
>
> *Color*: **Black**

13. Change the color to red and change the width to the third smallest.

14. Allow the counter to log information for a few minutes, and then click on the **Add Counters** button.

15. Select two more server counters to chart.

16. Be sure to chart the server counters using different line colors, line widths, or styles so that the parameters may be distinguished from each other.

17. After the counters have charted for a couple of minutes, delete them from the chart by highlighting them at the bottom of the window and pressing the **DELETE** key.

Charting allows a quick snapshot of the status of the network resources in real-time. This is helpful if the network is having problems and you are trying to diagnose the problem. The disadvantage to real-time data collection is that you probably will not be watching the Performance tool chart events until after a problem occurs.

Windows 2000 recognizes this and provides a tool called *Alert* that enables you to set thresholds for a selected counter. After the threshold is exceeded, an alert is issued. As an example, you will set a threshold for processor time, so that if the demands placed on it exceed 20%, an alert will be issued.

18. On the left side of the window, double-click on the **Performance Logs and Alerts** node.

19. Click on the **Alerts** icon.

20. Right-click in the right pane, and select **New Alert Settings...** from the menu choices.

21. When the *New Alert Settings* dialog box pops up, name the new alert **Processor Usage Alert**.

The *Alert Settings* dialog box will appear, as shown in Figure 21-5.

22. Click on the **Add** button to add a counter to the alert.

23. When the *Select Counters* dialog box appears, select the following counter:

> *Computer*: **Use local computer counters**
>
> *Performance Object*: **Processor**
>
> *Counter*: **% Processor Time**
>
> *Instance*: **_Total**

24. Click on the **Add** button, then click on the **Close** button.

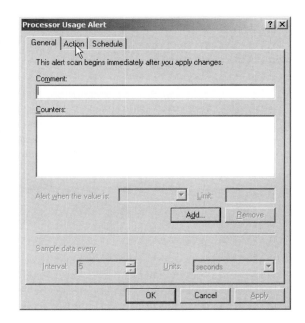

Figure 21-5: The Alert Settings Dialog Box

25. In the *Alert when the value is:* field, select **Over** from the drop-down menu.

26. Enter **20** in the *Limit* field.

27. Click on the **OK** button to apply the alert.

NOTE: Depending on the function of the computer you are using, you may need to alter the processor time.

28. Start a couple of application programs (a word processor and a spreadsheet, for example) so that the processor is placed under a load.

NOTE: By default, events are logged to the Application Event Log. To view these events, you must use the Event Viewer.

29. Navigate the *Start Menu/Programs/Administrative Tools/Event Viewer* path.

30. Click on the **Application Log** icon in the left pane, as in Figure 21-6.

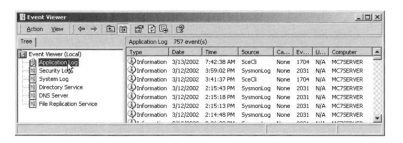

Figure 21-6: Clicking the Application Log Icon

You should see the alerts listed in the log. There will be events with the source set to *SysmonLog*, created by the Performance tool.

31. Double-click on an event with the source set to *SysmonLog*.

The *Event Properties* dialog box should appear, as in Figure 21-7. This is one of the events generated by the Performance tool based on the alerts you set up. It shows a description of the event, when the event occurred, and where the event originated.

32. Record the description in Table 21-1.

33. Click on the **OK** button to close the *Event Properties* dialog box.

Log is a Performance tool that captures counter data for a specified object over a long period of time. After the data is captured in a log, it may be viewed in one of the view types or exported into a spreadsheet.

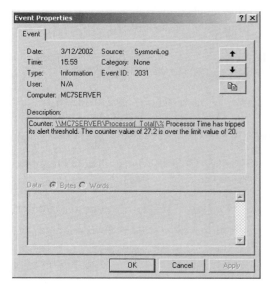

Figure 21-7: The Event Properties Dialog Box

Typically, a server experiences times of little activity and times of intense activity, and a long-running log will illustrate the peak and valley time periods, as well as place the server utilization in perspective. This is important so that an administrator does not overreact to the peak usage periods, or minimize the demands on the server simply because the only time data is collected is when the server is underutilized.

The following steps describe how to set up Log, and then export the collected data.

34. In the Performance tool, click on the **Performance Logs and Alerts** node in the left-hand pane, and then click on the **Counter Logs** icon.

35. Right-click in the right pane, and select **New Log Settings** from the pop-up menu.

36. Enter **Processor Usage Log** into the *Name* field and click on the **OK** button.

You should now see the *Processor Usage Log* dialog box, as shown in Figure 21-8.

37. Click on the **Add** button, and select the following counter:

> *Computer*: **Use local computer counters**
>
> *Performance Object*: **Processor**
>
> *Counter*: **% Processor Time**
>
> *Instance*: **_Total**

38. Click on the **Add** button, then click on the **Close** button.

At the bottom of the dialog box, there are two different settings: *Interval* and *Units*. These are used to set how often the log file will be updated.

39. Change the *Interval* field to **10**, and verify that the *Units* field is set at **Seconds**.

You must now tell Windows 2000 where to store the logged data.

40. Click on the **Log Files** tab.

41. Set the *Location* field to **C:\PerfLogs**.

42. Set the *File Name* field to **Processor_Usage_Log**.

Now you are ready to start the log.

43. Click on the **OK** button.

44. Right-click on **Processor Usage Log** in the right-hand pane and select **Start** from the pop-up menu to start creating the log file.

NOTE: Allow the log to capture processor data for a few minutes. If necessary, you may start an application to place the processor under a load, as before.

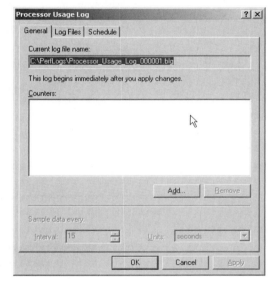

Figure 21-8: The Processor Usage Log Dialog Box

45. After the log has had time to acquire data, right-click on **Processor Usage Log** again and select **Stop** from the pop-up menu.

NOTE: To analyze the data acquired during the log session, you must return to the System Monitor.

46. Click on the **System Monitor** icon in the left-hand pane.

47. Click on the **View Log File Data** icon at the top of the chart window. The icon looks like a cylinder.

48. Navigate to the *C:\PerfLogs* folder and select the **Processor_Usage_Log_000001.blg** log file.

49. Click on the **Open** button.

You will be presented with an empty chart until you add the counter to the chart.

50. Click on the **Add Counter** button.

You will notice that you can only select the *% Processor Time* counter. That is because it is the only counter that was logged in your log file.

51. Select the **% Processor Time** counter.

52. Click on the **Add** button, and then click on the **Close** button.

The logged data will now be displayed in chart format, similar to the example in Figure 21-9. You may only want to observe relevant portions of the logged data, and the Performance tool lets you focus on any portion of the chart.

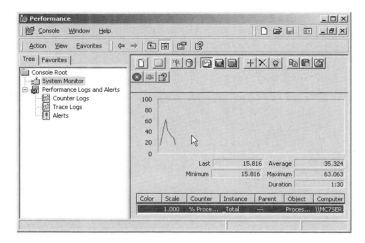

Figure 21-9: Viewing Logged Data as a Chart

53. Click on the **Properties** button in the toolbar.

54. Click on the **Source** tab in the *System Monitor Properties* dialog box.

At the bottom of the dialog box, you will see the *Time Range* options, as shown in Figure 21-10.

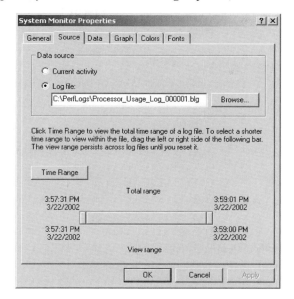

Figure 21-10: Setting the Time Range

55. Observe that the ends of the gray bar may be moved so that only a portion of the charted data is visible.

56. Click on the **Cancel** button.

Similar to the Chart display, *Report* displays real-time data captures as they occur. Whereas Chart contains historical data on a counter, Report updates the data at the prescribed interval, with each update overwriting the previous display.

To use Report, perform the following steps:

57. Change your data source back to the current activity by clicking on the **View Current Activity** button in the toolbar.

58. Click on the **View Report** button.

59. Add a counter as follows:

> *Computer*: **Use local computer counters**
>
> *Performance Object*: **Processor**
>
> *Counter*: **% Processor Time**
>
> *Instance*: **_Total**

Report will begin presenting the *% Processor Time* in the report screen.

The update period is set by default to five seconds. To change the update period, use the following steps:

60. Click on the **Properties** button in the toolbar.

61. In the *System Monitor Properties* dialog box, change the **Update automatically every** option.

TABLES

Table 21-1

| |
| |

LAB QUESTIONS

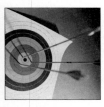

Feedback

1. What is the Performance tool used for?
2. What is the difference between an object and a counter?
3. Why is the Performance tool such an advantage in a network?
4. What are the steps for beginning a new chart?
5. Why is it a good idea to present the chart lines in different colors when logging more than one parameter?

Installing NetWare Client Software

Installation

OBJECTIVES

1. Install Netware Client.

RESOURCES

1. Network+ Certification Training Guide
2. Windows 2000 Professional workstation
3. Network connection to NetWare server
4. Novell Client Software CD
5. Admin password

DISCUSSION

In order to access a NetWare server from a client workstation, the client must have Novell's client software installed on it. During this Lab you'll perform the workstation install and log on to the server. You will also verify connectivity to the server.

Keep in mind that old software running on a Windows client will be detected and removed during the Novell Client installation. Examples of old software include Microsoft Client for NetWare Networks, Microsoft File and Print Sharing for NetWare Networks, and Microsoft Service for Novell Directory Services.

PROCEDURE

1. Boot the computer to the Windows 2000 desktop.

2. Insert the Novell Client Software CD.

A flash screen will appear. The window will look similar to Figure 22-1.

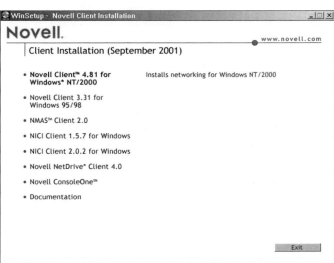

Installation

**Figure 22-1:
Flash Screen**

3. Click on the appropriate version of the client to install. For example, "*Novell Client 4.81 for Windows NT/2000.*"

4. Click on the **Yes** button to agree to the license agreement.

The Typical Installation radio button should be selected by default.

5. Click on the **Custom Installation** radio button, as in Figure 22-2.

6. Click the **Next** button.

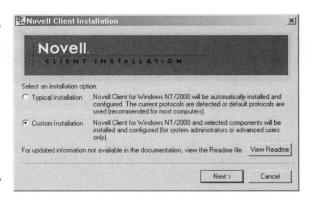

Figure 22-2: Installation Options

7. You will see the components to be installed listed with a check mark next to them. Record the default components selected in Table 22-1 and click on the **Next** button.

8. The next window will show available network protocols. The default selected is IP and IPX. Record the other three available options in Table 22-2 and click on the **Next** button.

9. Use the default NDS connection and click on the **Next** button.

10. Enter the name of your network tree. If you don't know it just leave the space blank and click on the **Next** button.

11. Click on **Finish**. Files will be copied and the client will be installed. At the end of the installation you will be prompted to reboot the computer. Click on the **Reboot** button.

Figure 22-3: The Login Screen

12. After the computer has restarted, you will be prompted to log in. Press **CTRL+ALT+DELETE** to log in.

13. Click on the **Advanced** button.

You will see a window similar to Figure 22-3.

14. Click on the **Trees** button, select the tree in your network, and click on **OK**.

15. Click on the **Contexts** button, select the appropriate context, and click on **OK**.

16. Click on the **Contexts** button, select the appropriate context, and click on **OK**.

17. Click on the **Servers** button, select the appropriate server, and click on **OK**.

18. Enter the administrator username, usually "*admin*", and the administrator password and click on **OK**.

19. The login process will commence and you can log in to the computer. If you are prompted to enter a username and password for the Windows 2000 login do so as prompted.

You can now test your connectivity to the server by viewing one of the volumes on the server.

20. Navigate the *Start/Run* path and enter the drive letter **F** followed by a colon (F:). This is the default drive letter assigned to the SYS volume on the server. You should see a window showing its contents.

21. Close all windows.

22. Click on the **Contexts** button, select the appropriate context, and click on **OK**.

23. Click on the **Contexts** button, select the appropriate context, and click on **OK**.

24. Click on the **Servers** button, select the appropriate server, and click on **OK**.

25. Enter the administrator username, usually "*admin*", and the administrator password and click on **OK**.

26. The login process will commence and you can log in to the computer. If you are prompted to enter a username and password for the Windows 2000 login do so as prompted.

You can now test your connectivity to the server by viewing one of the volumes on the server.

27. Navigate the *Start/Run* path and enter the drive letter **F** followed by a colon (F:). This is the default drive letter assigned to the SYS volume on the server. You should see a window showing its contents.

28. Close all windows.

TABLES

Table 22-1

Default Network Components

Table 22-2

Available Network Protocols

Feedback

LAB QUESTIONS

1. Why is it necessary to install NetWare Client software on workstations?
2. What is the default protocol of NetWare 6?
3. What is the default mapped drive letter for the volume SYS on a Novell server?

Creating NetWare User Accounts

OBJECTIVES

1. Set up a new user account in NetWare 6.
2. Test the new user account.

Networking

RESOURCES

1. Network+ Certification Training Guide
2. Windows 2000 Professional workstation
3. Network connection to NetWare server
4. Administrative access to server from a client

DISCUSSION

In the previous Lab Procedure you installed the client software on a Windows 2000 workstation. In this procedure you'll set up a user account on the server. Once the account is set up you'll test it to verify its functionality.

As with Windows NT, a client needs server space for work files. Typically, the space allotted to a user will be for personal work and for work that will be shared with others. Novell handles this by offering two methods for setting up user directories—*Data Directories* and *Home Directories*.

A Data Directory is used to store files that will be used by several members of the same group. These working directories, once created, can be made accessible to individual users, or groups of users, by making trustee assignments for the individual or group. A Home Directory is set up for a single user. These are files that the user doesn't intend to share with others.

In a typical file structure, the location of the home directories is set up under a parent directory that's normally called HOME or USERS. From HOME, individual users can be assigned to subdirectories. The normal convention is to name the subdirectory after the user's login name.

You'll create two user accounts in this Lab Procedure, and then create a home directory called USERS.

Networking

PROCEDURE

1. Log on to the workstation as **Administrator** or "admin".

2. From the workstation, navigate the *Start/Run* path.

3. Enter **z:\win32\nwadmn32**, where *z* is the mapped public drive on the server.

4. You will see the NetWare Administrator program, as shown in Figure 23-1. Close any tip screens that open.

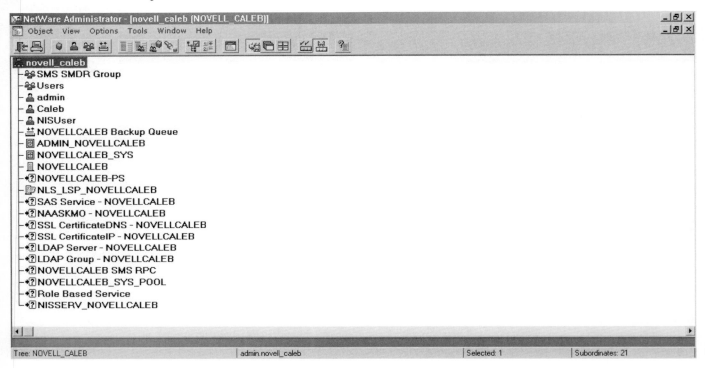

Figure 23-1: NetWare Administrator

5. Click the organizational unit for your server so that it is highlighted. Most likely it will be the first item in the list. It is the root object in the tree.

6. Click **Object/Create**. You will see a window similar to Figure 23-2.

7. Select Group for the class of the object and click on **OK**.

8. Enter a unique group name, such as the word Users, followed by your initials.

9. Click on the **Create** button and the group will be created.

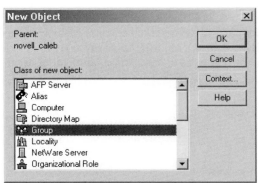

Figure 23-1: Create Object

10. As before, create a new object, but this time create a user. Name the User with a unique name.

11. For practice, create another user.

12. Record the Group Name and the User Names you created in Table 23-1.

13. From the main administrator window, double-click the SYS volume of the server. You will see the contents of the volume expanded.

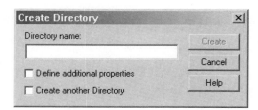

14. Click on **Object/Create**. You will be prompted to create a directory, as shown in Figure 23-3.

15. Enter a directory name identical to the Group name you created earlier and click on **Create**. The directory will be created.

Figure 23-2: Create a Directory

16. Highlight the group directory you just created, right-click on the icon, and select **Create**.

NOTE: You are now creating a subdirectory for each user.

17. Enter the name of the first user you created and click on **Create**.

18. Repeat the above steps to create another subdirectory for the second user you created.

NOTE: You could have created a home directory when you were creating the user by checking the Create Home Directory box in the Create User window. We are doing the same operation slightly differently.

19. Double-click on the first user you created. A user details window similar to Figure 23-4 will appear.

20. Click on the **Environment** tab.

21. Place the cursor in the Path field and click on the *Browse* icon on the right-hand side of the field.

22. Under *Browse Context*, double-click the SYS volume of the server.

23. Under *Browse Context*, double-click the users directory you created.

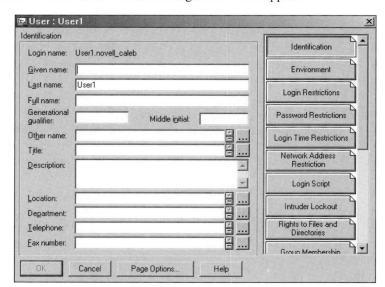

Figure 23-3: User Details

24. Under available objects you should see the two user directories you created. The window should look similar to Figure 23-5. Select the appropriate directory and click on **OK**.

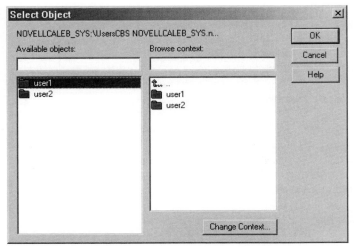

Figure 23-4: Selecting a Home Directory

NOTE: Assigning a home directory could also have been accomplished by checking the appropriate field in the Create User window.

25. The home directory will now be assigned. Record the information in the Volume field in Table 23-2.

26. In the user details window, click on the **Group Membership** tab.

27. Click on the **Add** button.

28. Under available objects, double-click the users group you created earlier. The user will now be added to the users group.

29. Click on the **Password Restrictions** tab in the user details window.

30. Uncheck **Allow user to change a password** and check **Require a password**.

31. Click on the **Change Password** button.

32. Type and retype a new password. Record the password you entered in Table 23-3 and click on **OK**.

33. Click on **OK** to the user details window and the changes will be applied.

34. Repeat the above steps to assign a home directory, group membership, and password to the second user you created earlier.

35. Close *NetWare Administrator* and log off the workstation.

36. Log on as the first user you created with the appropriate password to verify its functionality.

37. Log off and log on as the second user you created to verify its functionality.

38. Log off the workstation.

TABLES

Table 23-1

Table 23-2

Table 23-3

LAB QUESTIONS

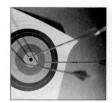

Feedback

1. How many objects did you create in this Lab?
2. What are two ways to create a home directory for a user?
3. What are two ways to add a user to a group membership?

Making Router Connections

Hardware Exploration

OBJECTIVES

1. Identify the components, cabling, and connections needed to route between two LANs.
2. Identify all rear panel port connections on a CISCO 1600 series router.
3. Identify the function and normal operation of status LEDs on a CISCO 1600 series router.
4. Properly connect the router in preparation for configuration.
5. Apply power to the router and determine if it has powered-up properly.

RESOURCES

1. One 10BaseT Ethernet LAN connection
2. One AUI LAN port
3. One ISDN BRI S/T connection
4. One ISDN phone connection
5. One fixed WAN port
6. One slot for a WAN interface card
7. Flash memory PC card
8. Console port for configuration from a terminal or PC
9. Security slot for Kensington-compatible lockdown cable
10. Autoinstall features for downloading configuration files

DISCUSSION

This Lab Procedure, and the next two, are concerned with internetworking. The concepts learned in the three experiments can be applied to a couple of situations. The first involves connecting two different networks, and the second involves a connection from a local network to an Internet Service Provider (ISP). The first scenario is illustrated in Figure 24-1.

Two networks are shown, East and West. Note that they are distinct networks because the network portions of their IP addresses differ. In order to connect the two LANs, routers are needed. The IP addresses that are assigned to the routers share the same network portion of the IP address.

Data leaving the routers is sent to a "modem." This may be an asynchronous dial-up modem, a T-Carrier CSU/DSU, or an ISDN adapter. The word modem is used loosely in the router experiments to mean any of the above devices. In practice, there's no such device as an ISDN modem. What the modem does is serve as an interface to the Public Switched Telephone Network (PSTN). Data delivered to the PSTN may use many technologies, such as analog transmission (circuit switched), Frame Relay, T1 (or higher), ISDN, ATM, or Packet Switching.

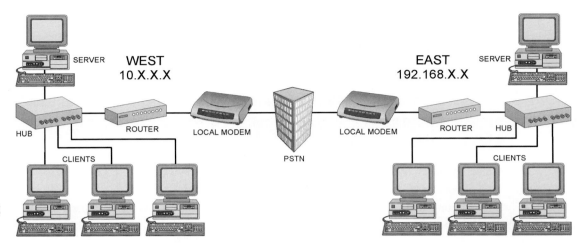

**Figure 24-1:
Interconnecting
Two Networks**

But a router will be needed to connect the two LANs because they have differing network addresses. A router will translate the differences between IP addresses by appending MAC addresses to TCP/IP packets. These MAC addresses are discarded along the way, and the MAC addresses of the devices passing the packet will replace the discarded MACs. However, at no time will the original source and destination IP addresses be removed.

The two routers shown in the illustration will maintain a list of MAC addresses and IP addresses used at their respective networks. When a packet arrives at either router, it will examine its routing cache, match the IPs in the packet, and accept the packet to the network. IP (or some similar network protocol) will route the packet to the correct node by matching its MAC and IP addresses. (Refer to Chapter 8 of Data Communications for a detailed discussion of address resolution.)

This scenario is common where a business has sites in various locations. The internetwork shown in Figure 24-1 may be one of several in a corporate intranet. The router is used to provide a connection between the various sites.

The second scenario is illustrated in Figure 24-2.

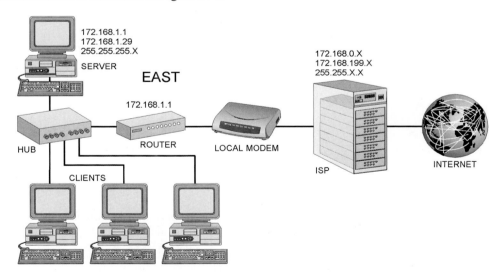

**Figure 24-2:
Interconnecting a
Network to an
Internet ISP**

In this situation, a LAN (East) is connected to the Internet through an ISP. Typically, the IP addresses for the LAN are leased from the ISP. Notice that the server has been assigned a block of 30 IP addresses, one of which has been assigned to the router. All 30 IPs are from the block of IP addresses made available from the ISP.

A router is needed in this situation so that all clients on the LAN can access the ISP. Normally, the router will be set up so that it's always in communication with the ISP, which makes Internet access available on-demand to the LAN clients.

Notice that in both examples, none of the clients or servers are actually connected directly to the router. The connection is made through a hub in both cases. When a user at a client computer in Figure 24-2 wants to connect to the Internet, a web browser (Netscape or Explorer, for example) is started. The browser has been configured to point to the IP address of the router. Once the router receives a request from the client, it forwards it to the ISP, and the download of data from the Internet (via the ISP) begins.

In a similar manner, when a client in Figure 24-1 wants to connect to the remote LAN, the remote is generally shown in Network Neighborhood as a named server. If the client has been given access to the server, the assigned user may click on it to see the specific machines connected to that server. And if he/she has been given access to any of the machines, clicking on that icon will gain access to files and directories on that particular machine.

The router in Figure 24-1 permits the connection of the networks. Access to services on the network, however, is set up at the server. A user on a local client that has been given access to the remote server may map a network drive to that server, place it on the desktop of the client computer, then click on it when a file is needed.

In this Lab Procedure, you'll identify the cabling, connections, and components needed to interconnect two "LANs." The LANs consist of a single PC on each end of the router connection. The router configuration you'll perform in the next Lab Procedure works equally well for connecting two actual LANs, but in order to minimize the time needed to set up the server and the clients, you'll simulate them with a simple computer on each end of the connection.

Connecting the LANs will be a CISCO 1600 series router that was specifically designed for LAN-to-WAN connections, as well as LAN-to-LAN connections.

PROCEDURE

A router is used to route data packets between different networks, that is, networks with different network IP addresses. The PCs that will be communicating across the internetwork will be configured with different IP addresses, and the routers will be used to reconcile the addresses so they can communicate.

First, let's get to know more about the router you'll be using. The CISCO 1601 router includes the following features:

- One Ethernet port using a 10BaseT connection or an AUI connection
- One fixed WAN port. Additional modules may be purchased for asynchronous, Frame Relay, ISDN, or X.25 connections.
- Flash PC card support
- Console port for configuration from a terminal or PC
- Autoinstall features for downloading configuration files

Hardware Exploration

The rear panel of the 1601 is shown in Figure 24-3.

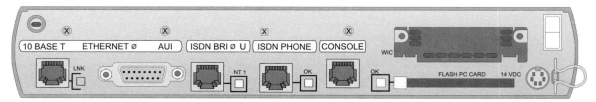

Figure 24-3: Rear Panel Connector Ports of the CISCO 1601 Router

PROCEDURE - 24

The function of each connection of the 1601 is shown in Figure 24-4.

CISCO 1601 ROUTER CONNECTIONS AND FUNCTIONS	
Label	**Function**
Ethernet 0 10BaseT	Connects the router to a 10BaseT Ethernet LAN through a hub or switch.
Ethernet AUI	Connects the router to an Ethernet LAN through a transceiver.
Console	Connects the router to a terminal or PC running terminal emulation software for configuration.
WIC	Slot for a WAN Interface card
Flash PC Card	Slot for the Flash PC card
ISDN BRI 0 U	Connects the router to ISDN services through an integrated NT1.
ISDN Phone	Connects an ISDN device, such as an ISDN telephone.

Figure 24-4: Connection Functions

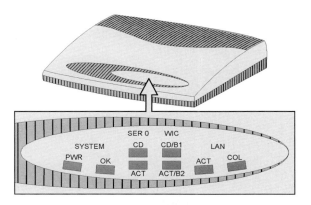

Figure 24-5 shows the front panel of the 1601 CISCO router. The panel includes LED status lights, which indicate various activities of the router. The functions of the LEDs are shown in Figure 24-6.

Figure 24-5: Front Panel Status LEDs of CISCO 1601 Router

CISCO 1601 ROUTER LED FUNCTIONS		
LED	**Color**	**Description**
System PWR	Green	DC power is supplied.
System OK	Green	Boot was successful; LED blinks during the boot.
LAN ACT	Green	Indicates data sent or received from Ethernet LAN.
LAN COL	Yellow	When flashing, indicates packet collisions on Ethernet connection.
BRI 0 B1	Green	An ISDN connection on B-Channel 1
BRI 0 B2	Green	An ISDN connection on B-Channel 2
WIC CD	Green	Active connection on the WAN Interface Card serial port.
WIC ACT	Green	Data is being sent over the WAN Interface Card serial port.

Figure 24-6: TCP/IP Properties Window

Figure 24-7 shows the installation of the router that you'll build.

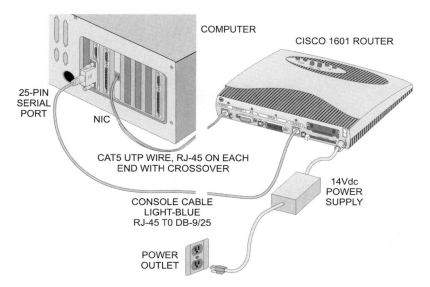

Figure 24-7: Connections Needed for Router Configuration

Observe the cable that is used between the 10BaseT Ethernet port on the router and the NIC in the PC. Since you'll be attaching single PCs to the router—and not to a hub—you must use a CAT5 UTP crossover cable for this connection.

The 10BaseT connector accommodates an RJ-45 connector and CAT5 UTP. In a normal network, it runs from the router to an available port on a hub. The hub serves as the central point for nodes to connect to the router. The serial port of the router connects to another router on a separate network. Notice that a null modem is installed between the serial ports of the routers. This is needed in order to cross over the connection between the two routers. Routers used in this type of situation may have been installed to separate a large LAN into smaller LANs in order to improve throughput and utilization rates.

Since the 1600 series routers offer several technologies for interconnecting networks, the serial port could also be used for a dial-up telephone connection to a remote router. In companies that have regional offices, this is frequently the case. A router is installed at the regional office and connected to a central site office. In addition to using the dial-up telephone network, the connection can be across an ISDN line, Frame Relay, or T-Carrier—when the appropriate WAN interface module is installed.

The console port is only used to configure the parameters of the router for the connection. Regardless of the type of connection, the configuration is entered via the console port. The router can be configured from any terminal, or from a PC running terminal emulation software. You'll be using HyperTerminal on a Windows PC for the configuration.

The connection runs between the Console port of the router and a serial port on the PC. When making the connection, be sure to use the light-blue cable with RJ-45 connectors. A separate adapter is needed on the PC side to connect the cable to either a DB-9 or a DB-25 serial connector.

The 14Vdc power is derived from a separate power supply that plugs into a 120Vac outlet. Power is applied with an ON/OFF switch located on the rear of the router, and next to the power cord connector.

1. Check to see that the power is OFF. If it is not, move the rocker switch down (to the 0 position) to turn it off, and follow the instructions below to make the connections, as shown in Figure 24-8.

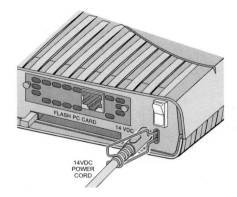

Figure 24-8:
Rocker Switch
Set to OFF

2. Connect the crossover cable to the NIC in the PC and to the 10BaseT port in the back of the router.

3. Take one end of the blue console cable and connect it to the DB-9 to RJ-45 console adapter that came with the router package, and connect the adapter to the serial port at the back of the computer.

4. Connect the other end of the blue console cable to the console port in the back of the router.

5. Connect the power cord to the 14Vdc input on the back of the router and slip the wire clip over the cord, as shown in Figure 24-9, to secure the power cord in place.

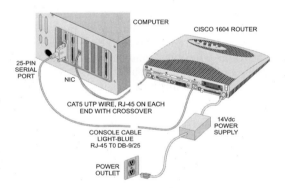

Figure 24-9:
Connect the
Power Cord

6. Plug the power supply into the wall socket.

7. Flip the power switch on the back of the router to the ON position.

If the unit is working properly, the LEDs on the front panel will appear as shown in Figure 24-10.

ROUTER PANEL LEDS	
Front Panel LED	**Description**
SYSTEM PWR	Will illuminate green when power is applied.
SYSTEM OK	Will illuminate green when system software is operational. This LED will blink as the router first goes through the boot sequence.
Rear Panel LED	**Description**
Flash PC OK	Illuminated green
10Base T LNK	Illuminated green

Figure 24-10: Front and Rear Panel LEDs

This Lab assumes you'll be setting up a connection between two networks using the router serial ports with a crossover between them. However, a router adds a tremendous amount of flexibility to a network and your instructor may have other plans. Before continuing, stop and check with your instructor for the configuration you'll be using.

LAB QUESTIONS

1. What is the purpose of the OK LED on the front panel of the router?
2. Which port on the rear of the router would be connected to an Ethernet hub using CAT5 UTP?
3. The SER 0 CD LED on the front panel of the router is lit. What does this mean?
4. What port on the rear panel of the router is used for entering configuration information?
5. Network A has a network address of 172.16.x.x, while Network B has a network address of 192.168.x.x. Is a router needed to connect these two networks? Why?

Feedback

Configuring a Router Connection

Software Exploration

OBJECTIVES

1. Enter the configuration parameters to a CISCO 1601 router to include the Ethernet IP address and the Serial IP address.
2. Specify RIP as the routing protocol.
3. Create a RIP routing table.
4. Password-protect the configuration.

RESOURCES

1. PC running Windows 9.x and HyperTerminal emulation software
2. CISCO 1601 router
3. Correct hardware connections as specified in Lab Procedure 23

DISCUSSION

In the previous Lab Procedure you connected the console port of the 1601 router to a serial port of a PC. In addition, you added a UTP crossover from the router's 10BaseT port to the RJ-45 port of the PC NIC. When powered on, the router booted with the SYSTEM PWR and SYSTEM OK LEDs illuminated as green. You're now ready to software-configure the router. To do so, you'll a terminal emulator. The HyperTerminal program that comes standard with Windows 9x is an ASCII emulator, and will be used for the configuration of the router.

Before beginning, you need to understand some of the specialized commands and syntax used with CISCO's command-line interface software called IOS. This is the router operating system. This Lab presents an overview of the commands, but you may want to take some time to read the CISCO IOS Basic Skills section of the **CISCO 1600 Series Software Configuration Guide**. In addition, the **Documentation CD** that comes with the 1601 router contains a considerable amount of information on configuration parameters. Finally, check out CISCO's web site at **www.cisco.com/** for more information.

Configuring a router isn't easy, which is why the above references were mentioned. Devices connected to the router or a typographical error in a configuration file may affect how it works (or doesn't work). Take your time when entering the data, double-check your entries, and use basic troubleshooting utilities such as ping to check connections.

The process begins by setting up a HyperTerminal session with the router, using the following settings:

- 9,600 bits per second
- 8 data bits
- No parity
- 1 stop bit
- Hardware flow control

The CISCO IOS configuration is composed of several layers. The structure of a command is defined by command modes. The command modes are:

- User EXEC
- Privilege EXEC
- Global configuration
- Interface configuration
- Router configuration
- Line configuration

During the configuration, you'll use each of these modes. You need to be able to move from one mode to the next, as well as have a basic idea of what each encompasses. The following describes each mode, and includes commands that will place you in another mode, or return you to a previous mode.

User EXEC: This mode begins when the router is first booted. It's identified by the prompt. One of the first actions you'll take is to give the router a name, and the name will then preface the EXEC prompt as in:

Router>

This identifies the name of the router as **Router**, and the > identifies the User EXEC mode.

User EXEC mode is used to change terminal settings, perform basic tests, and display system information.

Once you've finished working with the configuration, you leave the session by entering:

Router>logout

The **logout** command ends the session with the router.

Privileged EXEC: This mode is used to move to the configuration modes (Global, Interface, Router, and Line), so that the parameters of the router can be set up. The Privileged EXEC mode is identified with a # prompt. To enter Privileged Mode, enter:

Router>enable

Notice you must be in the User EXEC mode to move to Privileged EXEC. To leave the Privileged EXEC mode, enter:

Router#disable

This takes you back to the User EXEC mode.

Global Configuration: This mode is used to enter the specific configuration modes—Interface, Router, and Line. It's identified by the **(config)#** prompt. To enter Global Configuration, enter:

Router#configure

Notice that to enter Global Configuration, you must be in the Privileged EXEC mode.

When you enter Global Configuration using the configure command, the Interface Operating System (IOS) will ask you if you're configuring from a **terminal**, **memory**, or a **network**. For this Procedure, you'll always be configuring from a terminal (using the HyperTerminal emulation package). Since you'll always be using a terminal, you can skip the question by entering:

Router#config t

CISCO IOS commands can be implemented using partial commands. You have to enter enough of the command for IOS to recognize it as unique; hence, "**config t**" is actually "**configure terminal**". Experiment with partial commands a bit. The configuration you'll be entering uses them extensively, but you may want to collect your own shortcuts.

To leave all Configuration modes, enter **CONTROL-Z**. Look for this in the configuration file to be written as **CTRL-Z**, or as **^Z**.

Interface Configuration: This mode is used to configure parameters on the LAN and WAN interfaces. It's identified by the **(config-if)#** prompt. To enter the Configuration Interface mode, enter:

Router(config)#interface

Notice that you must be in Global Configuration mode to enter Interface Configuration.

Router Configuration: This mode is used to set parameters on the router, such as the routing protocol to run. It's identified by the **(config-router)#** command prompt. To enter Router Configuration, enter:

Router(config)#router [key word]

From the Global Configuration mode, you enter the Router Configuration mode. You must specify the parameter to configure by entering a keyword. For the most part, the keywords used are routing protocols such as **RIP, OSPF, BGP, IGRP**, and so on.

Line Configuration: This mode is used to set parameters of the terminal line. You'll use Line Configuration to set passwords on the configuration file. To enter Line Configuration, enter:

Router(config)#line [key word]

You enter Line Configuration from the Global Configuration mode. A keyword must be included with the line command. These include specifying the Terminal Controller (keyword: **tty**), Virtual Terminal (keyword: **vty**), and so on.

At any mode in IOS, you can enter a **?** to see a list of commands associated with that mode. You can also use the question mark for partial commands as in:

Router(config)#router question

This will return a list of keywords that can be used in the Router configuration. Assume, for example, that the list that was returned included the word **rip**. But what can you do with the router rip command?

Enter:

Router(config-router)#?

The screen will return an extensive list of router commands you can use.

You'll set up two passwords on the router, called **enable secret password** and **enable password**. The first is a very secure encrypted password, while the second is an unencrypted password. The idea behind the use of two passwords is that an intruder must have both to be able to reconfigure the router. The first will be difficult to obtain since it's encrypted.

The CISCO 1600 series routers store configuration settings in NVRAM (Non-Volatile Random-Access Memory). The command for saving the configuration is:

Router#copy running-config startup-config

If you don't save the settings to NVRAM, they won't be there the next time you power-up the router. Once the settings are saved, the screen will respond with **[OK]**. A shortcut for the save command is **copy run start**.

Save the settings frequently, exactly as you would when working with an application on a PC. This is a general overview of CISCO IOS. The best way to learn it is to work with it. So, let's dive in.

Software Exploration

PROCEDURE

1. Turn on the computer and bring up the HyperTerminal program.

2. In the *Connection Description* window, type **Router** and click on **OK**.

3. Select the serial Com port to connect to in the *Connect To* window, and click on **OK**.

4. In the *Port Settings* window, enter the following settings for communicating with the router, as shown in Figure 25-1:

    - Bits per second   **9600**
    - Data bits   **8**
    - Parity   **None**
    - Stop bits   **1**
    - Flow control   **None**

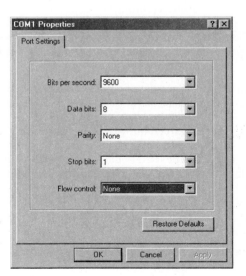

**Figure 25-1:
Port Settings
Window**

5. Click on **OK**.

6. Turn on the router.

The router's boot sequence will be displayed in the *HyperTerminal* window.

Starting the router with the default configuration settings

1. When prompted to enter the initial configuration, type **No** and press the ENTER key.

2. Press the ENTER key to begin communication with the router.

3. To enter the *Privileged EXEC* mode, type **enable** and press the ENTER key.

4. Type **erase startup-config** and press the ENTER key to clear any previous changes to the router configuration.

5. Press the ENTER key to confirm the erase command.

6. Type **reload** to reload the original configurations.

7. When prompted to proceed, press the ENTER key.

8. Type **No** and press the ENTER key when prompted to enter the initial configuration.

Configuring the router's hostname

1. Type **enable** to enter the *Privileged EXEC* mode.

2. Type **configure terminal** and press the ENTER key to enter the *Global configuration* mode.

3. Name the current host by typing **LAB-A**, and pressing the ENTER key.

4. Press the CTRL and Z keys to exit the *Privileged* mode.

5. Press the ENTER key to get a command prompt.

6. Type **copy run start** and press the ENTER key to save the configurations to *NVRAM*.

7. Press ENTER when prompted for a filename to accept the default.

Configuring the Router's Interface

Ethernet interface

1. When the command prompt reappears, type **config t** (shortened version of the configure terminal command) and press the ENTER key to enter the *Global configuration* mode.

2. Type **int e0** to prepare the router to accept *Ethernet* configurations and press the ENTER key.

3.   Type **192.168.0.43 255.0.0.0** and press the ENTER key.

4.   Type **no shutdown** and press the ENTER key.

5.   Press the CTRL and Z keys.

Serial interface

1.   Type **config t** and press the ENTER key.

2.   Type **interface Serial0** and press the ENTER key.

3.   Type **ip address 172.168.20.2 255.255.0.0** and press the ENTER key.

4.   Type **no shutdown** and press the ENTER key.

5.   Press the CTRL and Z keys.

Configuring the routing protocol

1.   Type **config t** and press the ENTER key.

2.   Type **router rip** and press the ENTER key.

3.   Type **network 10.0.0.0** and press the ENTER key.

4.   Type **network 172.168.0.0** and press the ENTER key.

5.   Press the CTRL and Z keys.

This sets the routing protocol to be run on the network.

Configuring the routing tables

1.   Type **config t** and press the ENTER key.

2.   Type **ip host LAB-A 192.168.20.1 172.168.20.2** and press the ENTER key.

3.   Type **ip host LAB-B 10.147.7.1 172.168.20.1** and press the ENTER key.

4.   Press the CTRL and Z keys.

Essentially, you have created the routing tables for the routers. They will collect MAC addresses for these IPs and then will be able to route packets accordingly.

Configuring the Line Settings

Line con 0

1.   Type **config t** and press the ENTER key.

2.   Type **line console 0** and press the ENTER key.

3. Type **password cisco** and press the ENTER key.

4. Type **login** and press the ENTER key.

5. Press the **CTRL** and **Z** keys.

Line vty 0 1

1. Type **config t** and press the ENTER key.

2. Type **line vty 0** and press the ENTER key.

3. Type **password cisco** and press the ENTER key.

4. Type **line vty 1** and press the ENTER key.

5. Type **password cisco** and press the ENTER key.

6. Press the **CTRL** and **Z** keys.

7. Type **copy run start** and press the ENTER key.

8. Type **show run** and press the ENTER key to show the configuration settings.

9. Enter the *User EXEC* mode and type **logout** and press the ENTER key to exit the configuration session.

10. Turn the power to the router off, wait 30 seconds, and turn it back on.

11. From HyperTerminal, enter the *Privileged EXEC* mode and type **show run**.

12. Verify that the configurations you entered have been saved to NVRAM.

13. Configure the *LAB-B route*r in the same manner as above, using the following information:

Hostname	LAB-B
Ethernet ip address	192.168.20.1 255.255.255.0
Serial interface	172.168.20.2 255.255.0.0
Router protocol	router rip
Network ip	192.168.20.0
Network ip	172.168.0.0
Ip host A	192.168.20.1 172.168.20.2
Ip host B	10.147.7.1 172.168.20.1
Line con 0	password cisco
Line vty 0	password cisco
Line vty1	password cisco

Feedback

LAB QUESTIONS

1. What command do you use to switch from *Privileged EXEC* mode to *User EXEC* mode?
2. While in *User EXEC* mode, what command do you enter to go to the *Privileged EXEC* mode?
3. Which configuration mode do you enter to specify the IP address of the Ethernet port?
4. What command do you enter to save a configuration?
5. What command do you enter to view the current configuration?

Routing Across Two Networks

**Software
Exploration**

OBJECTIVES

1. Assign network consistent IP addresses to LAB-A and LAB-B computers.
2. Use the Ping utility to check all connections from LAB-A.
3. Use the Ping utility to check all connections from LAB-B.

RESOURCES

1. Fully configured CISCO 1601 routers
2. Serial crossover cable
3. Two computers running Windows 9x

DISCUSSION

Now that you've configured routers for internetworking, it's time for the acid test: Do they work? One of the most effective tools for testing network connections is ping.

In the following procedure, you'll ping each IP address that you set up in the configuration. If the ping is successful, it means that the router is configured properly and capable of routing packets between the networks.

Before beginning, refer to Figure 26-1 for the IP addresses of the two computers. You must assign IP addresses to the computers before assuming the network will operate.

You may, as an option, set up shares between the two computers connected by the routers.

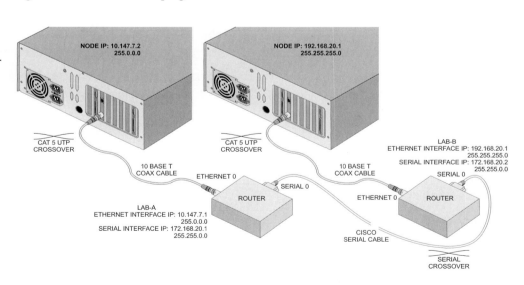

Figure 26-1: IP Addresses of Two Computers

**Software
Exploration**

PROCEDURE

1. At each of the client computers, go to *Control Panel* and double-click the *Networks* icon to bring up the *Network properties* box.

2. For the client computer connected to the LAB-A router, enter the following IP address: 10.147.7.2.

3. For the client computer connected to the LAB-B router, enter the following IP address: 192.168.20.2.

4. Restart each client computer.

5. From the LAB-A client computer, bring up an MS-DOS command prompt window.

6. In Table 26-1, enter the IP addresses of each device listed.

7. Ping each device using the Ping command and the IP address.

    Example: Type **ping 10.147.7.2** and press the ENTER key.

8. Enter the results of each ping in Table 26-1.

9. Enter the IP address addresses of each device listed in Table 26-2.

10. From the LAB-B client computer, repeat steps 6 through 8.

11. Enter the results of each ping in Table 26-2.

TABLES

Table 26-1: LAB-A Ping Results

LAB-A PING RESULTS		
Network Components	IP Address	Ping Result
LAB–A PC		
LAB–A Ethernet Interface		
LAB–A Serial Interface		
LAB–B Serial Interface		
LAB–B Ethernet Interface		
LAB–B PC		

Table 26-2: LAB-B Ping Results

LAB-B PING RESULTS		
Network Components	IP Address	Ping Result
LAB–B PC		
LAB–B Ethernet Interface		
LAB–B Serial Interface		
LAB–A Serial Interface		
LAB–A Ethernet Interface		
LAB–A PC		

LAB QUESTIONS

1. What's the purpose of the serial crossover cable?
2. What function does the ping command perform?
3. Since the network will route ping packets, will this configuration also work for a LAN connected in place of each of the client computers?
4. Suppose that a third network needs to be connected to the LAB-A and LAB-B routers. How can it be done?

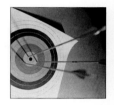

Feedback

Creating and Using Tags in Web Documents

Software Exploration

OBJECTIVES

1. Use the following HTML header tags: <html>, <head>, <title>, <body>, <h1>, and <p>.
2. Create an HTML document and vary the format with the following tags: <em>, <cite>, <kbd>, <strong>, <b>, <u>, and <i>.

RESOURCES

1. Network+ Certification Training Guide
2. Windows 2000 Professional workstation
3. One formatted 3.5-inch floppy disk
4. Internet access

DISCUSSION

HTML is an abbreviation for Hypertext Markup Language. It provides a way to code a document so that it can be displayed on the World Wide Web area of the Internet.

The web operates independently of the type of computer connected to it. For example, a web document looks the same no matter if it's viewed from an IBM computer or an Apple computer. The TCP/IP protocol suite allows for machine independence, while HTML allows for document independence on the web.

Many of the files you may have viewed on the Internet have been encoded with HTML, or a combination of HTML and a commercial HTML editor. Newer versions of commercial word processors also include HTML translators so that you can create a document using Microsoft Word or WordPerfect, and save it as an HTML file. The codes are added during the save. Then, if you open it in a web browser, it will appear as if you had added all the HTML codes.

An HTML file is essentially a plain text document with specific commands added so that it can be viewed on the web. Windows *Notepad* is a plain text editor. You'll use *Notepad* to create HTML documents in this, and several of the following Lab Procedures.

Markup tags are used to HTML encode a document. Tags specify the structure, or look, of a document. There are tags indicating the start of a paragraph, for headings, for creating items in lists, for linking to other documents, and so on.

Create Web Pages Using HTML

HTML is a method of encoding plain text so that it can be displayed in a Web browser on the Internet.

HTML tags are identified by placing the coding script in angle brackets.

Figure 27-1: Text in a Web Browser

Figure 27-1 shows a simple HTML page as it appears in a web browser such as Netscape or Internet Explorer. Figure 27-2 shows the same document with the HTML tags included.

Notice that all tags are enclosed in angle brackets. Angle brackets are an HTML requirement, and are used to let the browser know that the command within the brackets contains information on how to display text.

The first tag is <html>. (HTML is not case sensitive. You may encode using either upper or lower case letters.) This tag is used when beginning an HTML file and signifies that the information to follow is to be displayed according to HTML commands. All web documents begin with the <html> tag.

The next tag is <head>. It's used to identify the header of the document. You may have noticed that some documents printed from the Internet contain a name in either the top left or right corner. The name is created by using the <head> tag.

Conventionally, the <head> tag is also used for specifying the title of the web page. In Figure 27-2, the browser is instructed to display it as a title with the <title> command. Now, when the page is printed, the title—the name given to the document with the <head> tag—will be displayed at the top of the page. Notice that following the title is the tag </title>, and following this is the tag </head>. The backslash used with the command marks the end of an instruction to the browser.

The <body> tag specifies the beginning of the web page. Notice that the </body> tag doesn't occur until the end of the document. In other words, the <body> and </body> tags bound the content that will appear when the page is opened in a browser.

```
<html>
<head>
<title> HTML Tags </title>
</head>
<body text="#000000" link="#0000ff" vlink="#551a8b" alink="#ff0000" bgcolor="#c0c0c0">

<h1>Create Web Pages Using HTML</h1>


<p>HTML is a method of encoding plain text so that it can be displayed in a Web browser on the
Internet.


<p>HTML tags are identified by placing the coding script in angle brackets.
</Body>
</html>
```

Figure 27-2: HTML Source Code

In Figure 27-2, there are several text commands immediately following the <body> tag. These specify the colors of the text, background, links, and so forth. We'll take a closer look at these later in this procedure.

The page begins with a heading, marked by the <h1> tag. The <h> tag will be displayed as large, usually bold, text by the browser. There are six heading fonts available with HTML: h1, h2, h3, h4, h5, and h6. The font will be smaller as the number increases, but all are normally displayed in bold. It's acceptable to repeat numerical values in the heading tag, but don't skip any, because this may confuse the browser, and the heading may be displayed like the rest of the text.

Figure 27-3 illustrates the effects of assigning header tags. The first "Create Web Pages Using HTML" was created with a h1 tag, while the last heading was created with a h6 tag. The end of each heading is marked by the </h> tag.

A paragraph of text is marked with a <p> tag. The tag tells the browser to indent the first line (usually five spaces) and to begin the next line at a left-justified margin. The right margin will wrap to the next line regardless of where it ends in a word. There are HTML commands to avoid this but most browsers automatically wrap lines. In an early version of HTML, a paragraph was ended by including a </p> tag. Beginning with version two of HTML, this requirement was dropped.

```
<html>
<head>
<title> HTML Tags </title>
</head>
<body text="#000000" link="#0000ff" vlink="#551a8b" alink="#ff0000" bgcolor="#c0c0c0">

<h1>Create Web Pages Using HTML</h1>

<h2>Create Web Pages Using HTML</h2>

<h3>Create Web Pages Using HTML</h3>

<h4>Create Web Pages Using HTML</h4>

<h5>Create Web Pages Using HTML</h5>

<h6>Create Web Pages Using HTML</h6>

<p>HTML is a method of encoding plain text so that it can be displayed in a Web browser on the Internet.

<p>HTML tags are identified by placing the coding script in angle brackets.

</body>
</html>
```

Figure 27-3: Effects of the Heading Tag

You may, however, include the </p> tag if it helps you keep track of each paragraph. It has no effect on how the file is displayed. When you need to start another paragraph, simply begin the first line with <p>. Figure 27-4 summarizes the basic HTML tags described in the preceding paragraphs.

HTML DOCUMENT HEADER TAGS	
<html>	This signifies the beginning of a document to be displayed in a browser.
<head>	The beginning of a header, this is typically the title of the document.
<title>	This is the filename of the document.
<body>	This marks the beginning of the text that will appear in the browser.

Figure 27-4: Document Header Tags

You may wonder why it's necessary to master basic HTML encoding when there are many commercial products available that do much of the work for you. First, use off-the-shelf HTML editors wherever you can. It saves time and reduces errors because HTML encoding is particularly meticulous. Once you have prepared the basic document, open it in an ASCII text editor (*Notepad*) so that you can revise or massage it to suit your specifications. And, undoubtably, you will want to make changes in backgrounds, font colors, or link paths to other parts of the page.

In this Procedure, you'll begin in *Notepad* and create a personal web page. All of the tags described above will be used. Later, you will add to the personal page so that, gradually, a reference of HTML tags is created.

**Software
Exploration**

PROCEDURE

1. Open *Notepad* in Windows.

2. Under File, select **New**.

3. Realize that, unless directed otherwise, directions in an HTML page that are italicized require you to enter specific information, such as your name.

   For example, if your name is John Smith, a markup written as:

   > <title>*Your first name Homepage*</title>

   would be entered as:

   > <title>*John's Homepage*</title>

4. Enter the following text:

   > **<Html>**
   > **<Head>**
   > **<title> (Your first and last name)</title>**
   > **</Head>**
   > **<Body>**
   > **<h1> (Your first name) Homepage</h1>**
   > **<p>I take classes at (Name of your school). This is my first HTML document.</p>**
   > **</Body>**
   > **</html>**

5. When you've finished, choose **Save As** under the File heading. Save the file as (the first, middle and last initial of your name) **html.txt** to a floppy disk.

For example, if your name is John Adam Smith, save the file as jashtml.txt.

6. **Exit** the *Notepad* program.

7. Start your **web browser** (Netscape, Internet Explorer, or equivalent).

8. Once it's loaded, go to the **File** menu and choose **Open File**.

9. Select your floppy drive.

10. For Type Of File in the *Open* dialog box, select **txt** for text file.

11. From the list of text files, locate the one with your initials, click on it, and choose **Open**.

12. Observe the file you created in *Notepad*, which should now be displayed on the browser screen.

It will contain all of the HTML tags that you added to the text. To view it without seeing the tags, it must be designated as an HTML file.

13. Go to the **File** menu again, but this time choose **Save As**.

14. Use the same filename as you did in *Notepad*, but change the txt extension to **htm**.

Personal computers permit you to use only three characters in filename extensions.

15. Save the htm file to the disk.

All web browsers will still recognize the file as HTML, with the htm extension.

16. Click on the **OK** button.

17. Go to the **File** menu once again, and this time open the htm file you saved to the disk.

The HTML version of the *Notepad* file will now be displayed on the screen without revealing the tags. However, in order for HTML to be successful as a document, you may need to provide the web browser with instructions on how to present words or phrases on the screen. These directions are called formatting tags. The portion of a document that is tagged is referred to as an element. The sentences within a paragraph are elements. A heading is an element. The title of a document is an element. Any part of an HTML document bound with tags is an element.

There may be elements within an element. Consider the following sentence:

<p>I <b>love</b> creating HTML documents.

This sentence is a brief paragraph bound by <p>. It's an element. However, the paragraph contains another element, "love", bound by <b> and </b>. The <b> tag (for bold) is an HTML markup command that will cause a word or phrase to appear in bold print.

There are no restrictions to adding elements inside of elements, other than the effect they may have on the reader of a web document. Usually, simple is best.

Creating elements is a key factor to writing effective HTML code. Formatting provides you with an array of tools to enliven and enrich a web page; but keep in mind, if it is used inappropriately or excessively, the reader of your page will become confused—and cruise to another site.

Figure 27-5 shows an HTML file in which the text has been manipulated using several formatting tags.

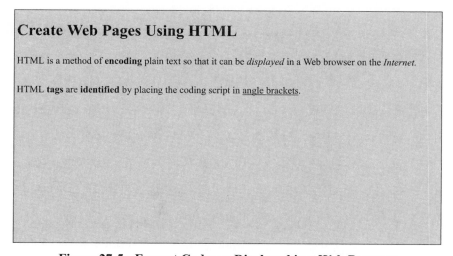

Create Web Pages Using HTML

HTML is a method of **encoding** plain text so that it can be *displayed* in a Web browser on the *Internet*.

HTML **tags** are **identified** by placing the coding script in <u>angle brackets</u>.

Figure 27-5: Format Codes as Displayed in a Web Browser

The HTML formatting codes for the document are included in Figure 27-6.

```
<Html>
<Head>
<title> HTML Tags </title>
</Head>
<body text="#000000" link="#0000ff" vlink="#551a8b" alink="#ff0000" bgcolor="#c0c0c0">

<h1>Create Web Pages Using HTML</h1>


<p>HTML is a method of <b>encoding</b> plain text so that it can be <em>displayed<em/> in a Web browser on the
<cite>Internet</cite>.

<p>HTML <kbd>tags</kbd> are <strong>identified</strong> by placing the <i>coding</i> script in <u>angle brackets</u>.

</Body>
</html>
```

Figure 27-6: HTML Formatting Codes

The first tag used is <b>, which causes an element to appear in a web browser as bold text. The word "displayed" is bound by the <em> tag that may either bold an element, or cause it to appear in italic text. In this example, the effect is to italicize the text. <cite> is another command that causes the text to appear in italics, as does the tag <i>.

An interesting tag is <kbd> (keyboard), which makes text have an appearance like computer-generated ASCII text. It's typically used to indicate the response a computer makes to a keyboard input and looks similar to the font used in older DOS and UNIX machines. Sometimes keyboard is used to indicate, in a series of web-based instructions, the text or commands an operator is to enter with the keyboard.

The <strong> tag is used to emphasis a word or phrase and it usually interpreted by a browser as a bold command. As you can see in the figure, <strong> has the same effect as <b>.

The <u> tag causes an element to be displayed as underlined text. In the figure, the phrase "angle brackets" will be underlined because it is bound by <u> and </u>.

Figure 27-7 summarizes the formatting commands presented in this discussion. The rest of this Procedure will provide you with an opportunity to try each of these commands, then to view their effect on the browser you're using.

Figure 27-7: Summary of HTML Formatting Tags

HTML FORMATTING TAGS	
Command	**Result**
<b>	Bold: This text appears as **Bold**.
<em>	Emphasis: This text appears as **Emphasis**.
<cite>	Cite: This text appears as *Cite*.
<kbd>	Keyboard: This text appears as `Keyboard`.
<strong>	Strong: This text appears as **Strong**.
<i>	Italic: This text appears as *Italic*.
<u>	Underline: This text appears as <u>Underline</u>.

18. Go to *Notepad* and open the **personal web page** you've begun.

19. Scroll to the end of the document and add the following:

<p>I <em>really</em> enjoy the Internet.

The tag <em>, for "emphasis," is usually displayed in a browser as bold text. Shortly, you'll view the effects of several tags in the Netscape browser.

20. Add the following line beneath the one above:

<p>One day I may write a book called <cite>A Guide To Writing HTML</cite>.

The <cite> tag, for "citation," will italicize words bound by the tag. In this example, we've cited the title of a book, and we want the browser to display it properly.

21. Add this sentence to the *Notepad* file:

<p>I would write the book by using my <kbd>keyboard</kbd>.

The <kbd> tag will usually display text as it appears on a plain text terminal screen. It's useful if you want to include a computer program in an HTML document and want it to appear exactly as it would to a person entering the program.

22. Now, add the following sentence:

<p>It would be a <strong>great</strong> book!

The "strong" tag directs the browser to give the word "great" additional emphasis. Most browsers respond by bolding words bound by the <strong> tags.

23. For the purpose of comparison, enter the same sentence but replace <strong> with the bold tag, **<b>**:

<p>It would be a <b>great</b> book!

24. On occasion, you may need to italicize a word. Type the following:

<p>It would be a <i>rewarding</i> experience.

25. At times, you may want to underline a word or phrase. Enter the following:

<p>I think I <u>will</u> write an HTML book.

26. Once all of the tagged sentences have been added to your personal web document, save the file (using a txt extension) and exit *Notepad*.

27. Start your **web browser**.

28. Once it's loaded, open the txt file from *Windows Notepad*.

29. Save the file with the same name but change the extension to **htm**.

You'll be asked if you want to replace the existing file—the htm file you created earlier in this lab.

30. Click on **Yes**.

31. Open the HTML version of the file from the disk.

32. Compare the HTML tags used in the txt file with the effects they produced on the htm file. Record the results in Table 27-1.

33. Save both the **txt** and **htm** files to the floppy disk.

TABLES

Table 27-1

Tag	Effect

Feedback

LAB QUESTIONS

1. Is an HTML version of a *Notepad* file displayed on the screen with or without revealing the tags?
2. Which HTML commands display bold text?
3. What was the difference in appearance between text using the <strong> tag and the <b> tag?
4. What was the difference in appearance between text using the <cite> tag and the <italic> tag?

Creating and Using Lists in Web Documents

Software Exploration

OBJECTIVES

1. Describe the difference between unordered, ordered, and definition lists.
2. Use the following tags to create lists: <ul>, <ol>, <dl>, <dt>, and <dd>.
3. Create HTML lists, display the lists in a web browser, and print the documents.

RESOURCES

1. Network+ Certification Training Guide
2. Windows 2000 Professional workstation
3. One formatted 3.5-inch floppy disk
4. Internet access

DISCUSSION

Information is what the Internet is all about. In order to get the information, it must be presented in a manner that makes it easy for the viewer to read. A common technique used to do this is to present the information as a series of lists. Think of a list on the Internet as a table of contents. Typically, the items in a list are linked to other documents, or they may contain links to sections within a document. Of course, a list may also be used to simply list items without using links.

In this activity, you'll add three types of lists to the personal web page you're compiling in *Notepad*—unordered, ordered, and definition lists.

An unordered list displays items with a bullet. To begin an unordered list, start the list with the markup <ul>, which stands for unordered list. Each item in the list is preceded with the tag <li>, for list item. When the list is complete, add the tag </ul> to let the browser know it has ended. An example of an unordered list is shown in Figure 28-1. In this simple example, the three types of HTML lists have been placed in an unordered list.

- Unordered List

- Ordered List

- Definition List

Figure 28-1: Example of an Unordered List

As you can see, each item is prefaced with a bullet. Figure 28-2 shows the HTML tags used to create the list. The browser is told that an unordered list follows with the tag <ul>. Next, each item in the list is indicated with the <li> tag. The browser is told that the list is completed by adding the </ul> tag at the end of the list.

```
<html>
<head>
<title> HTML Tags </title>
</head>
<body text="#000000" link="#0000ff" vlink="#551a8b" alink="#ff0000" bgcolor="#c0c0c0">

<ul>
<li>Unordered List
<li>Ordered List
<li>Definition List
</ul>

</body>
</html>
```

Figure 28-2: HTML Unordered List Tags

Let's go to *Notepad* and add the unordered list to your personal web page.

Software Exploration

PROCEDURE

1. Go to *Notepad* from Windows.

2. Open your personal web page.

3. Add the following list to the end of the document. Fill in the blanks with pertinent information about yourself.

    > **<p>Here are some interesting things about me:**
    > **<ul**
    > **<li>My favorite hobby is ____ .**
    > **<li>My favorite sport is ____ .**
    > **<li>My favorite food is ____ .**
    > **</ul>**

4. Once you've finished, **save** the file and **exit** *Notepad*.

5. Start your **web browser**.

6. Open your personal homepage.

7. Save it as an **htm** file.

8. When the browser prompts you if you want to replace the existing file, click on **Yes**.

9. Open the HTML version in the browser.

10. Carefully examine the items to ascertain that they are displayed in a bulleted list. Then, **save** the HTML file to your floppy disk.

An ordered list allows you to number each item in the list. For this reason, you may see references to ordered lists as **numbered** lists.

The tag for an ordered list is <ol>. Each item in the list is proceeded with the tag <li>. Once the list is complete, it ends with the tag </ol>.

An example of an ordered list is shown in Figure 28-3.

1. Unordered List

2. Ordered List

3. Definition List

Figure 28-3: Example of an Ordered List

By making a simple change in the list tag, all items are displayed in numerical order. Look at Figure 28-4, and notice that in the coding, the list items aren't numbered. If numbers had been added to the coded version of this list, they would be duplicated when the document was viewed in a browser.

As you can see, each item in the list is tagged with <li>, as it was in an unordered list.

11. If necessary, open your personal web page in *Notepad*.

12. Add the following to the document. Fill in information about yourself in the blanks.

```
<html>
<head>
<title> HTML Tags </title>
</head>
<body text="#000000" link="#0000ff" vlink="#551a8b" alink="#ff0000" bgcolor="#c0c0c0">

<ol>
<li>Unordered List
<li>Ordered List
<li>Definition List
</ol>

</body>
</html>
```

Figure 28-4: HTML Ordered List Tags

```
<p>Here are some interesting things about me:
<ol>
<li>My favorite hobby is ____.
<li>My favorite sport is ____.
<li>My favorite food is ____.
</ol>
```

13. Once you've finished, **save** the file and **exit** *Notepad*.

14. Start your **web browser**.

15. Open the *Notepad* text file in the browser, and save it with the **htm** extension.

16. Choose **OK** when asked if you want to replace the existing file.

17. Open the htm version of the file into your browser.

18. Are the list items now numbered? Record the results in Table 28-1.

19. Save the file with the **htm** extension and with the **txt** extension to your disk.

A definition list contains a term and a description of the term. It begins with the markup <dl>, for definition list. The term to be described is tagged with <dt>, for definition term. The description of the term is tagged with <dd>, for definition description. Once the list is finished, it ends with </dl>. An example of a definition list being displayed is shown in Figure 28-5.

Definition List
    A definition list contains a term and a description of a term.

Figure 28-5: Example of a Definition List

An example of the tags used for definition lists are shown in Figure 28-6. Notice that the convention followed is similar to the other list types.

```
<html>
<head>
<title> HTML Tags </title>
</head>
<body text="#000000" link="#0000ff" vlink="#551a8b" alink="#ff0000" bgcolor="#c0c0c0">

<dl>
<dt>Unordered List
<dd>A list of bulleted items.
<dt>Ordered List
<dd>A list of numbered items.
<dt>Definition List
<dd>A term and a description of the term.
</dl>

</body>
</html>
```

Figure 28-6: HTML Definition List Tags

A definition list contains a term and a description of the term. More than one term may be defined within a single set of definition tags by alternating <dt>, <dd>; <dt>, <dd>;<dt>, <dd>; and so on before ending the list with </dl>.

Figure 28-7 contains all tags associated with unordered, ordered, and definition lists.

HTML LIST TAGS	
Unordered List Tags	**Appears in Browser As**

`<ul>`
`<li> Item 1`
`<li> Item 2`
.
.
.
`<li> Item X`
`</ul>`
	• Item 1
	• Item 2
	.
	.
	.
	• Item X

Ordered List Tags	**Appears in Browser As**

`<ol>`
`<li> Item 1`
`<li> Item 2`
.
.
.
`<Li> Item X`
`</ol>`
	1. Item 1
	2. Item 2
	.
	.
	.
	X. Item X

Definition List Tags	**Appears in Browser As**

`<dl>`
`<dt> Term 1`
`<dd> Definition of Term 1`
`<dt> Term 2`
`<dd> Definition of Term 2`
.
.
.
`<dt> Term X`
`<dd> Definition of Term X`
`</dl>`
	Term 1
	   Definition of Term 1
	Term 2
	   Definition of Term 2
	.
	.
	.
	Term X
	   Definition of Term X

Figure 28-7: HTML List Tags

20. Open your personal web page in *Notepad*.

21. Add the following definition list to the document:

```
<dl>
<dt>Unordered List
<dd>A list of bulleted items.
<dt>Ordered List
<dd>A list of numbered items.
<dt>Definition List
<dd>A term and a description of the term.
</dl>
```

22. Once you've finished, **save** the file and **exit** *Notepad*.

23. Start your web browser.

24. Open the text version of your personal web page.

25. Save the text file as **htm**.

26. When the browser asks if you want to replace the existing file, click on **Yes**.

27. Open the **htm** version of the file from the disk.

28. Check the file to ascertain that it does indeed contain a list of terms and their descriptions. Record the descriptions of the first five terms in Table 28-2.

29. Save the file with the **txt** extension and the **htm** extension to your disk.

TABLES

Table 28-1

Table 28-2

Term	Description

Feedback

LAB QUESTIONS

1. Did your htm version of the file contain the expected list of terms and descriptions?

2. Does an ordered list contain bullet lead characters, or numeric lead characters?

3. What type of lead character is present in a definition list?

4. What is the overall purpose of using lists in an HTML document?

Creating and Using Links in Web Documents

OBJECTIVES

1. Use the <href=> tag to directly create links.
2. Use the <href=> tag to indirectly create links.

Software Exploration

RESOURCES

1. Network+ Certification Training Guide
2. Windows 2000 Professional workstation
3. One formatted 3.5-inch floppy disk
4. Internet access

DISCUSSION

The most valuable aspect of HTML is the ability to link documents. On a web browser, a word or phrase that's highlighted and/or underlined represents a link. HTML links may be established to any address on the Internet.

In this activity, you'll create two types of links—URL links (also called indirect links) and direct links. A URL link, when activated, will take you to another web site, probably on another server. Direct links may be made to other documents on the same server and in the same directory.

Direct links are quite valuable when initially setting up a web site, and for organizing a large number of files on a site. Suppose you develop networking SOPs that will be placed on an internal web site. A direct link can be set up between the procedures that allows a user to go from one to the other simply by clicking a linked procedure title or number. Small web sites are created using direct links as well. The site may have several pages along with several graphics. When the files are uploaded to an ISP, they're direct linked and the ISP administrator places them in the same directory on the ISP server. This way, the administrator will not have to manipulate the tags you placed in the documents.

We'll begin with URL links. You'll practice by using the personal homepage you've worked with for all HTML encoding. Document links won't be explored in this Procedure because most commercial word processors contain tools for linking sections of a document.

Recall that a URL (Universal Resource Locator) is used to identify specific addresses of documents on the World Wide Web. Since the addresses are maintained in the files of servers and routers on the Internet, they are used as reference points for navigating the web. In other words, a URL is as close as you get to a reference anchor on the Internet.

Each link is tagged with the <a> markup, for "anchor." There are several ways to initiate a link in HTML but the <a> tag will notify the browser that a link is to follow. Immediately following the <a> tag is the <href=> (hypertext reference) tag. Next comes the URL address, which is the reference for the link.

The browser must also be told how the link will be initiated—by highlighting some text, by inserting an image, and so on. This action is stated in the anchor, as well.

This is an example of a link to the Marcraft homepage:

Let's go to the <a href="http://www.owt.com/marcraft/">Marcraft homepage.</a>

The <a> tag identifies the markup as a link. The href= indicates a hypertext reference to a URL. The complete URL is bound by quotes. It's important to include the beginning and ending quotes, and good form to include the forward slash at the end of the address. Following the address is the section of text that will initiate the link, Marcraft homepage. Notice that the text is between angle brackets, and the markup ends with </a>.

Let's try using URL anchors with your homepage and see what happens.

Software Exploration

PROCEDURE

1. Open your personal homepage in *Notepad*.

2. Add the following:

    <p>A good source of technical information is the <a href="www.cisco.com/">CISCO</a> Web site. <p>For information about NT software, visit <a href="www.microsoft.com">Microsoft.</a>

3. Save the file in *Notepad*.

4. Open the text version of the file in your browser.

5. Save the file as **htm**.

6. Connect to the Internet.

7. Open your htm homepage file from the disk.

8. Is the link "CISCO" highlighted? Record your answer in Table 29-1.

9. Click on the link.

10. Describe what happened in Table 29-2.

11. Click the **Microsoft** link.

12. Describe what happened in Table 29-3.

Anchors are also used to directly link documents. A direct link is used to connect documents with unique file names that reside on the same server and in the same directory. For example, a document may refer you to another file on the same server for more information.

To link files on the same server in the same directory, all that's required is to include the file name in the link anchor. For example, let's assume two files, file-a.htm and file-b.htm. At a key word in file-a, we want to link to file-b.

The HTML coding in file-a would appear as:

For more information, go to <a href="file-b.htm">file-B.</a>

Notice that the syntax used is identical to that used for a URL link. However, the file name is used in place of the URL. The tags used with direct and indirect links are summarized in Figure 29-1.

HTML DIRECT AND INDIRECT LINK ANCHORS	
Link Type	**Appears in Browser As**
URL (Indirect) Links Used to link to another web site <a href= *"name of web site to link to">word or phrase that will launch the link*</a> Example: <P>Click <a href= "www.microsoft.com">here</a> to go to Microsoft's web site.	Click **here** to go to Microsoft's web site.
Direct Links Used to link to another document on the same server and directory <a href= *"name of file to link to">word or phrase that will launch the link*</a> Example: <P>For more information, see the <a href= "Appendix.htm">Appendix.</a>	For more information, see the **Appendix**.

Figure 29-1: HTML Link Anchors

13. Start a new document in *Notepad*.

14. Using the HTML tags introduced earlier, create a document that includes the following paragraph, titled File-A:

    <p>This is File-A and it's linked to <a href= "file-b.htm">< File-b></A>. File-B contains information about creating direct links.

15. Save the file to your disk using the filename **file-a.txt**.

16. Select **New** under the File drop-down menu.

17. Using HTML tags introduced earlier, create a document that includes the following paragraph titled File-B:

    <p>This is File-B and it's linked to <a href= "file-a.htm" >File-A</a>. Links are created using an anchor and a href tag.

18. Save the file using the name **file-b.txt**.

19. Open both files in your web browser, and save both to your disk as **htm** files.

20. Open **file-a.htm** in your browser.

TABLES

Table 29-1

Table 29-2

Table 29-3

Feedback

LAB QUESTIONS

1. When you open file-a.htm in your browser, is the File-B link highlighted?
2. Click the File-B link, and describe what happens.
3. Is the link to File-A highlighted when you open file-b.htm in your browser?
4. Describe what happens when you click on the File-A link.

Using Images in Web Documents

**Software
Exploration**

OBJECTIVES

1. Insert a graphic into an HTML document using the <img src=> tag.
2. Incorporate images with the text in an HTML document by aligning the image to the bottom of the text, top of the text, at the right margin, and at the left margin.
3. Adjust the width and height of an image.
4. Insert an image that links to another site.

RESOURCES

1. Network+ Certification Training Guide
2. Windows 2000 Professional workstation
3. One formatted 3.5-inch floppy disk
4. Internet access

DISCUSSION

Images can add appeal as well as enhance the functionality of a web page. They can also overwhelm the viewer if they are overused, or if they are used inappropriately. How much is too much?

If text can do the job more efficiently, then use text; if an image saves the user time, use it. Web surfers expect a certain amount of graphics due to their reliance on Windows-based software and the graphical appeal of the web in general. And, there are some graphic elements that seem to be taken for granted, such as buttons, scroll bars, and so on.

Images are added with the img markup. This is followed by the src tag, which is followed by the URL of the image. For example, to add an image of a blue ball, the tag looks like: <img src=blueball.gif>

It's one thing to insert an image in a HTML document and another to put it where you want it to be. This can be tricky, but the image markup can be combined with an align tag that helps in the placement. By default, an image will be aligned with the bottom of a line of text. In the example shown above, the bottom of the blue ball will align with the bottom of any text surrounding the ball.

You can indicate the location of an image by specifying the alignment. Options that are available with the align tag are shown in Figure 30-1.

For example, to align an image so that the top of the image is aligned with the top of the line of text, the markup looks like: <img src=image.gif align=top>

HTML IMAGE AND ALIGNMENT TAGS	
Tags	**Appears in a Browser As**
Image Tag <img src=*filename of the image*>	An image tag written in this manner defaults to the bottom of the line of text.
Alignment Tags <img src=image.jpg align=bottom>	Bottom: The bottom of the image aligns with the bottom of the line of text. This is the default specification and needn't be specified.
<img src=image.jpg align=top	Top: The top of the image aligns with the bottom of the next line of text.
<img src=image.jpg align=middle>	Middle: The middle of the image aligns with the bottom of the next line of text.
<img src=image.jpg align=left>	Left: The image is on the left margin, and text flows around it.
<img src=image.jpg align=right>	Right: The image is on the right margin, and text flows around it.

Figure 30-1: HTML Image and Alignment Tags

The specification of the alignment is indicated with the equal sign. For the HTML pages you create in these activities, follow the syntax as shown in the above example. However, a word of caution—the alignment tag may be written before the src tag, or after, as shown in the example. It shouldn't make a difference, but if you have trouble using it as shown, try inverting the positions of the src and align tags.

Now go to your personal web page in *Notepad* and try the markups for positioning images.

Software Exploration

PROCEDURE

1. Go to *Notepad* and open your personal web page file.

2. Add the following lines to the file:

   <p>This line contains an <img src=image.gif> image.
   <p>The top of this <img src=image.gif align=top> image is aligned with the text on this line.
   <p>The middle of this <img src=image.gif align=middle> image is aligned with the bottom of the line of text.
   <p>This <img src=image.gif align=left> image is placed on the left margin.
   <p>This <img src=image.gif align=right> is placed on the right margin.

3. **Save** the file and **exit** *Notepad*.

4. Start your browser, and open the text version of your file.

5. Save it as an **htm** file. Then, open the HTML version of your web page.

6. Take a close look at the sample image as it appears in your document.

7. Determine if the alignment is as described in the text surrounding the image. Record the results in Table 30-1.

8. Save both the text and htm versions of your page.

In addition to specifying the placement of the image, you should also tell the browser the size of the image. Image size is specified according the width and height in pixels. Typically, if you specify a size other than the actual size of an image, it will be scaled by the browser to fit your dimensions. However, be sure to experiment a bit before placing an extraordinarily large image on a web site.

The image attribute looks like: <img src=image.gif width=50 height=25>

You may also include placement tags in the container. For example, to align the above image with the right margin, the tag is written as: <img src=image.gif align=right width=50 height=25>

9. Go to *Notepad* and open your personal web page again, if necessary.

10. Add the following to the page:

    <p>This image<img src=image.gif width=25 height=12> is small.
    <p>This image<img src=image.gif width=35 height=25> is larger.
    <p>This image<img src=image.gif width=70 height=45> is even larger
    <p>This image<img src=image.gig width=95 height=65> is really big.
    <p>But this image<img src=image.gif width=150 height=100> is the biggest.
    <p>This medium-sized image<img src=image.gif width=75 height=50 align=top> is aligned with the top of this line.
    <p>This really big image<img src=image.gif width=200 height=150 align=middle> is centered to the bottom of this line of text.

11. Save the file and **exit** *Notepad*.

12. Start your browser, and open the text version of your page.

13. Save the file as an **htm** document.

14. Open the HTML version, and take a close look at the size attributes of the images.

15. Compare the size attributes to the dimensions specified in the HTML tags. Record the results in Table 30-2.

16. Determine the effect that the alignment specifications have on the size attributes. Record the results in Table 30-3.

Images are frequently used as links to other sites. The effect is that when you click on a linked image, you're taken to another server, or the link may lead to another document on the same server/directory

Image links are used to connect to a different URL, as well as to link to documents on the same server/directory. When you go to a web site, you begin at the homepage of the site. It will include links to other areas of the site and, at times, these will be represented with a graphic that's descriptive of the area. For example, to send an e-mail to the site, you may be required to click a mailbox.

An example of an image used as a link to another URL is:

> <p>This is an image link <a href="http://www.netscape.com/"><img src=image.gif></a> to another site address.

When viewed in a web browser, the sentence contains a graphic that, when clicked, connects to the Netscape homepage. Notice that the technique is to include the image element within the anchor. Size and placement attributes of the image can also be specified in the image element.

17. Go to *Notepad* and open your personal homepage.

18. Using HTML, encode the following in your file:

> **One of the greatest museums in the world is the Smithsonian Institution, located in Washington, D.C.**
> **Want to go?**
> **Then buckle your seatbelt, click on the graphic, and let's go!**

NOTE: *Use image.gif for the graphic with width=200 height=200.*
The URL for the Smithsonian is www.si.edu/

19. Once you've finished, **save** the file, and **exit** *Notepad*.

20. Start your browser, open the text file, and save it as an **htm** file.

21. Open the HTML file and determine if the graphic was included in the file. Record the results in Table 30-4.

22. Click on the graphic and observe what happens. Record the results in Table 30-5.

23. Save both the text version and the htm version of the file to your disk.

TABLES

Table 30-1

Table 30-2

Table 30-3

Table 30-4

Table 30-5

LAB QUESTIONS

Feedback

1. What is the tag that will place the file image.jpg on a page and align it to the right?
2. What tag is used to insert the file image.jpg and shrink it to a size of 200×125?
3. What tag is used to insert the picture file image.jpg as a hyperlink to the web site www.yahoo.com?
4. Write a tag that will insert the file image.jpg that is currently located in C:\pub\binaries\pictures\?

Using Colors in Web Documents

OBJECTIVES

1. Examine the RGB Hex Triplet Color Chart.
2. Experiment with text color markup tags.
3. Combine color and formatting tags.
4. Identify default colors and know how to change them.
5. Specify or change the color of the text on documents or visited links.

**Software
Exploration**

RESOURCES

1. Network+ Certification Training Guide
2. Windows 2000 Professional workstation
3. One formatted 3.5-inch floppy disk
4. Internet access

DISCUSSION

You may have noticed that each time you opened the HTML version of your web page, the text and background colors didn't change. The background is gray, links are blue, and a visited link changes to purple.

These are default colors used with HTML. Unless another color is specified in the code, these same colors will always appear in your browser. What if you don't like these colors? Then change them. But first, you'll need to know what colors are available.

HTML is very specific concerning color schemes. Many of the commercial HTML editors provide wide latitude in implementing them so that you can create about any color you want. In fact, an excellent chart is maintained on the Internet that shows the full range of colors you can select from. Let's begin by visiting this site.

PROCEDURE

1. Connect to the Internet.

2. In the address window, enter the following URL:

    http://quasar.un1.edu/tutorials/rgb.html

**Software
Exploration**

This should take you to the RGB Hex Triplet Color Chart. The chart shows all 216 color values. The various tones, or shades, of each color are obtained by mixing the colors red, green, and blue. The colors are "mixed" by combining six hexadecimal numbers. The six hex numbers used are: 00, 33, 66, 99, CC, and FF.

For example, orange is specified with the combination FF6600.

Colors are specified in the rigid order of red, green, and blue. In the example for the color orange, FF (decimal 255) is red, 66 (decimal 102) is green, and 00 (decimal 0) is blue. This produces a color with a heavy red component, medium green component (nearly yellow), and no blue value. Figure 31-1 lists several other examples.

EXAMPLES OF RGB HEX COLORS	
Hex Number	Color
FF0000	RED
00FF00	GREEN
0000FF	BLUE
FF00FF	PURPLE

Figure 31-1: Examples of RGB Hex Colors

To change the color of text within a paragraph, use the <font color= xxxxxx> tag preceding the text that you want to change. End the tag with </font>. These tags are typically placed immediately following the <body> tag, but as you'll see shortly, they can be inserted anywhere in the document.

Get ready to insert a paragraph into your homepage and vary the color of your text.

3. From *Notepad*, open the text file of your personal homepage.

4. Add the following to your homepage:

   <p> While I like <font color=FF0000> red </font>, my favorite color is <font color=0000FF> 0 blue </font> instead.
   <p> On occasion, I may give up <font color=0000FF>blue </font> for <font color=00FF00>green </font> unless I decide I like <font color=CCCCFF> mauve </font> instead.
   <p> There is, of course, a range of colors in between such as <font color=FF6600> orange</font>, <font color=CCFF00> purple </font>, and <font color=66FF00> greenish-yellow</font>.

5. **Save** the file and **exit** *Notepad*.

6. Open the file in your browser and save it as **htm**.

7. Open the HTML file, and determine if your paragraph contains a variety of colors. Then, record the results in Table 31-1.

8. Save the text file to your disk.

You can use the font color markup with other text tags such as <strong>, <cite>, or <underline>. Include the color tag within the format markup. For example, <cite color=FF0000> will change the color of text in italics to red.

The font tag is normally used for small sections of text within a document. It adds emphasis to an area of text. To change the color of all the text in a document, or for links, color tags are placed in the body markup, as shown in Figure 31-2.

```
<html>
<head>
<title> HTML Tags </title>
</head>
<body text="#0000FF" link="#0000ff" vlink="#551a8b" alink="#ff0000" bgcolor="#c0c0c0">

<H1>Change the Color of All the Text</h1>

<p>HTML allows the <b>coloring</b> of plain text so that it can be <em>displayed<em/> in a Web browser on the
<cite>Internet</cite> in any shade desired.

</body>
</html>
```

Figure 31-2: HTML Formatting Codes for Text Color

The following steps will give you practice manipulating colors in the text.

9. Using HTML, create, and encode a paragraph in your personal web page.

10. Use the RGB color chart to select a color close to those specified.

NOTE: The color of the text is specified as [color=blue], while the end of the color is specified as [/color].

11. Once you've finished, open the text file and save it as **htm** back to your disk.

HTML default colors are a gray background, black text, and blue links. When a link has been visited, it changes color to purple. A gray, black, and blue screen isn't particularly colorful. Many of the web pages you've seen contain much brighter color schemes.

HTML colors include 216 [color=red] colors [/color]. The text can be changed to [color=white] white [/color], [color=green] green [/color], [color=light green] light green [/color], [color=dark green] dark green [/color], or [color=yellow green] yellow green [/color].

There's also a full range of [color-red] reds [/color] such as [color=purple red] purple red [/color], [color=dark red] dark red [/color], [color=orange red] orange red [/color], [color=light red] light red [/color], [color=pink] pink [/color], or [color=green-red] dull red [/color].

In this procedure, you'll vary the color of your personal web page. All 216 colors are available, but you'll probably discover that some combinations work better together than others.

12. In *Notepad*, open the text version of your personal web page.

13. Locate the <body> tag near the beginning of the document. If your page doesn't have a <body> tag, refer to previous examples for its placement in the document.

14. Determine if there are any colors specified in the body tag. Record the results in Table 31-2.

If no colors are specified in the <body> tag, HTML defaults to gray, black, and blue. Keep in mind that the <body> tag is inclusive of the entire HTML file; if a markup is placed with the body tag, the complete file will be affected.

To change the color of the background, specify the color in the body tag using the hexadecimal color scheme. Refer to the RGB Hex Triplet Color Chart.

Background colors are specified using the bgcolor=xxxxxx tag.

For example: <body bgcolor=6666FF> will change the color of the background.

15. In the *Notepad* version of your personal homepage, change the body tag to **<body bgcolor=FF6600>**.

16. **Save** the text file, and **exit** *Notepad*.

17. Open your text file in your browser, and save it as an **htm** file.

18. Open the HTML version of your homepage.

19. Observe the color of the background. Record the results in Table 31-3.

Text colors may also be changed by specifying a color in the body markup. However, some care must be taken when specifying the background and text colors. For example, don't make them the same color or close in value. If you do, you won't be able to read the text.

20. Specify the text color by using the text=xxxxxx tag in the body markup.

For example, <body text=0000CC> will produce blue text.

21. Open your personal web page in *Notepad*.

22. Change the body tag to **<body bgcolor=FF6600 text=6666FF>**.

23. **Save** the file and **exit** *Notepad*.

24. Open the text version of your web page in your browser.

25. Save it as **htm**.

26. Open the HTML version of your page.

27. Observe the color of the text. Record the results in Table 31-4.

All links within the document are also specified in the body tag. HTML provides several options and we'll concentrate on two that are commonly used.

The first is the color of a link. This is done with a link tag. For example: <body link=110000> will display links as dark red. It's normally a good idea to also specify the color of a link that has been visited. This helps the reader keep track of followed links.

A visited link uses a vlink tag. For example, <body link=110000 vlink=FF0000> will display links as dark red, but once the link has been clicked, the color will change to a bright red.

28. From *Notepad*, open your personal web page.

29. Change the body tag to the following:

        <body bgcolor=FF6600 text=6666FF link=33FF00 vlink=FFFFFF>

30. Save the file and **exit** *Notepad*.

31. Open the text file in your browser, and save it as **htm**.

32. Open the HTML file.

33. Observe the color of the links. Record the results in Table 31-5.

34. Click on a link, then return to your homepage.

35. Observe the color of the link, now that it has been visited. Record the results in Table 31-6.

The Internet is rich with wonderful graphics and innovative techniques for linking, organizing, and sharing information. This Lab Procedure has only been an introduction to HTML that may prove to be helpful to you when editing code generated from a commercial HTML editor.

Perhaps the best way to learn how to create web documents is to study the source code of sites that you find useful and appealing. Web browsers come equipped with drop-down menus that allow you to see the tags used with each site you visit. Essentially, the webmasters of these sites are allowing you to learn their craft by observing what has worked for them. But that's a sort of trademark of the Internet; the sharing of knowledge and the promise that all of us will have the opportunity to contribute to a revolutionary communication medium.

TABLES

Table 31-1

Table 31-2

Table 31-3

Table 31-4

Table 31-5

Table 31-6

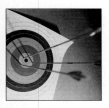

Feedback

LAB QUESTIONS

1. Code the following two short paragraphs with HTML code in *Notepad*, then save them as htm files. The first file, File-1, is to be linked to the second file, File-2. File-2 is also to be linked to File-1.

File-1

Linking is an important advantage of documents posted on the Internet. With an understanding of how to link documents on the same server, anyone with access to that server can easily retrieve information. More about linking can be found in File-2.

File-2

Linking allows anyone with Internet access to browse information posted on web sites. Information about direct links can be found in File-1. By linking to remote servers, you can easily navigate the globe with just a few mouse clicks. A good source for more information about these techniques is the CISCO web site.

NOTE: Notice that File-2 contains the name "CISCO". You're to include a link to the CISCO web site using the company name as the link.

Configuring TCP/IP Clients

OBJECTIVES

1. View the available protocols.
2. Configure the TCP/IP protocol on a client.
3. Specify TCP/IP tools to be used.

Networking

RESOURCES

1. Network+ Certification Training Guide
2. Windows 2000 Professional workstation
3. Server and client IP address information

DISCUSSION

Windows 2000 supports several networking protocols. A networking protocol is a set of rules or conventions used on a network that allow nodes to communicate in a reliable manner. The networking protocols supported are:

- IPX/SPX
- NetBEUI
- TCP/IP
- DLC
- AppleTalk
- Remote Access Services

IPX/SPX (Internetwork Packet Exchange/Sequenced Packet Exchanged) was originally developed by Xerox Corporation and forms the basis of Novell NetWare. Novell had established a substantial presence in the networking market prior to Windows 9x and NT/2000. Because of this, it's the default network protocol installed when Windows 9x is set up.

It offers the advantage of being a routable protocol. This means that data packets include headers identifying the node's address in a wide area network. A node can then send data packets to any other network that offers similar capabilities in interpreting Network layer headers.

NetBEUI (Net-BIOS Extended User Interface) is a network protocol developed by IBM for smaller LANs, those with fewer than 200 nodes. On the plus side, NetBEUI is a fast and simple network protocol to implement and, since it's been around for almost fifteen years, is extremely reliable. Many smaller LANs routinely use NetBEUI as the networking protocol.

On the negative side, however, NetBEUI isn't routable. This means that if the LAN that it's installed on needs to communicate with nodes on another LAN, the communication won't occur without some intervening protocol; and if the users on the LAN will need Internet access at some point in the future, the protocol will need to be changed to a routable protocol (IPX or TCP/IP).

TCP/IP (Transmission Control Protocol/Internet Protocol) has been used reliably for several decades on the Internet, and is capable of transporting packets to any LAN, no matter the machine types—as long as the remote LAN is also running TCP/IP. Unlike the other protocols described in this section, it's not proprietary, it spans the Network and Transport layers of the OSI Reference Model, it supports several levels of reliability, and it is almost universally used in wide area networks. IP is deployed at the Network layer, and is noted for the use of IP addresses. An IP address is assigned (permanently or dynamically), and is unique for all machines running TCP/IP. Since the addresses are unique, a node may communicate with any remote node that also has a unique IP address. The IP represents a logical address that interconnects any two nodes.

Windows 2000 provides direct support for administering IP addresses in two tools called WINS and DHCP. WINS (Windows Internet Naming Service) is used to resolve computer names to IP addresses. When a client is configured, you must name the computer. If this client also has an IP address, WINS will resolve the client's computer name to its IP address. This saves you the trouble of trying to remember IPs for dozens of clients. DHCP (Dynamic Host Configuration Protocol) is used to dynamically assign IP addresses to clients. The idea is that not all clients will need an IP address at the same time, or for the same amount of time. IP addresses are becoming a commodity, and DHCP allows them to be used by the client on an as-needed basis.

DLC (Data Link Control) is a subset of IBM's SDLC (Synchronous Data Link Control), and is typically used when clients are connecting to large IBM mainframes. Unless the clients are part of an IBM-equipped shop, use TCP/IP.

AppleTalk is the network protocol used with Macintosh computers. Windows 2000 allows Macintosh clients to launch and share Macintosh-formatted files stored on a 2000 server.

RAS (Remote Access Service) allows users to dial-in to an NT service from a remote, and typically temporary, location such as their home, a motel, or an airport. It's also used for dial-up Internet access by running TCP/IP over a PPP (Point-to-Point Protocol) connection between the client and ISP access server.

Host is the user name of the client computer. This name is usually the same as the computer name. Domain is the Internet domain name of the server that the client is connected to. Note that this name will probably be different than the domain name of an NT/2000 server—the two have different meanings.

DNS Server Search Order is a field that allows the client to access more than one server using DNS. The client will try the first IP when resolving a domain name, but if it's busy, will go to the second IP. The advantage to having more than one DNS server is that you'll be connected more quickly because the IP-to-domain name resolution will occur faster.

This Lab Procedure contains step-by-step instructions for configuring TCP/IP in a client PC. Of the networking protocols described above, TCP/IP is the only one that will run on all client operating systems that Windows 2000 supports. These include Windows 3.1, 3.1x (Workgroups), 95, and 98; MS-DOS clients, OS/2 clients, Apple Macintosh clients, and clients running UNIX.

As with the previous Lab Procedure, you'll be required to document the setting changes you make to the client. This is not only a good networking practice, but it also provides you with a list of particulars about the client in the event you have to troubleshoot it at a later time.

PROCEDURE

1. Complete the information in Table 32-1 for the TCP/IP properties assigned to your computer. Ask your instructor for the appropriate information.

2. From the Windows 2000 desktop, navigate the *Start/Settings/Network/Dial-up Connections* path.

Networking

3. You will see a window with a list of current connections. Right-click on the **Local Area Connection** icon and select **Properties**.

4. Record the components listed in Table 32-2.

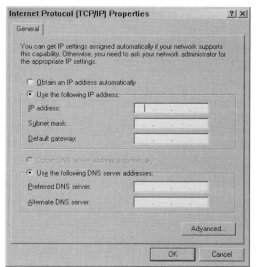

5. Click the **TCP/IP Protocol** and click on the **Properties** button. You will see a window similar to Figure 32-1.

6. If the IP address is automatically obtained by DHCP, write Yes in Table 32-3. Record the appropriate information regarding your IP address, subnet, gateway, and DNS addresses in Table 32-3.

7. Click on the **Advanced** button. You will see a window similar to Figure 32-2.

Figure 32-1: TCP/IP Properties

8. Click on the **WINS** tab and record the address, if any, of the WINS servers in Table 32-3.

9. Record any other information that is available on the other tabs of the Advanced TCP/IP Settings window in Table 32-3.

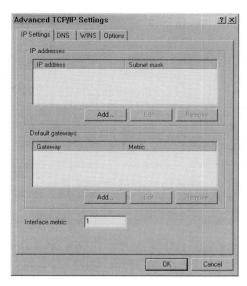

Figure 32-2: Advanced TCP/IP

10. Click on the **Cancel** button for both *Advanced* and *TCP/IP* Settings.

11. While TCP/IP is still highlighted in the *Local Area Connection Properties* window, click on **Uninstall**.

12. You will be given a warning. Click on **Yes** to confirm the uninstall.

13. You will be prompted to restart the computer. Click on **Yes** to do so.

14. You will be prompted to select at least one protocol for the connection to work. Click on the **No** button to select a protocol later.

15. After the computer has restarted go to the *Local Area Connection Properties* window as before.

16. Click on the **Install** button. Select **Protocol** and click on the **Add** button.

17. Select the **Internet Protocol TCP/IP** and click on **OK**. TCP/IP will be installed.

18. From the *Local Area Connection* properties window click on **TCP/IP** and click on the **Properties** button.

19. Using the information in Table 32-3, enter the appropriate settings in the window.

20. Click on the **Advanced** button and enter the appropriate settings using Table 32-3.

21. Click on **OK** to both the *Advanced* and *TCP/IP Properties* windows.

22. Close the *Local Area Connection Properties* window.

23. Try testing your network connectivity by viewing a web page on the Internet (if available) or browsing the network neighborhood.

TABLES

Table 32-1

INSTRUCTOR SPECIFIED SETTINGS	
IP address automatically obtained by DHCP?	
IP Address	
Subnet Mask	
Default Gateway	
DNS Servers	
WINS Servers	

Table 32-2

COMPONENTS LISTED

Table 32-3

INDIVIDUAL COMPUTER SETTINGS	
IP address automatically obtained by DHCP?	
IP Address	
Subnet Mask	
Default Gateway	
DNS Servers	
WINS Servers	
Other	

LAB QUESTIONS

1. What is the default setting for using DHCP in Windows 2000: Enabled or Disabled?

2. Is it necessary to have a WINS server set to browse Network Places?

3. What is the difference between the host and the domain?

Feedback

Using TCP/IP Utilities

OBJECTIVES

1. Using a Windows 9x client and NT server, explore the following TCP/IP utilities:

ARP
NBTSTAT
NETSTAT
FTP
Telnet
Tracert
IPConfig
Ping

**Software
Exploration**

RESOURCES

1. Network+ Certification Training Guide
2. Windows 2000 Professional workstation
3. Access to a LAN running TCP/IP
4. Access to the Internet

DISCUSSION

The TCP/IP networking model includes a variety of tools that can assist you in troubleshooting networking problems. In this Laboratory Procedure, you'll initiate several common utilities. Not all utilities are available on Windows client computers, and, depending on the structure of the network they're run on, not all are available on a server.

A Windows NT or Novell NetWare server offers the broadest range of utilities for you to experiment with. But you should also implement them at client workstations because their appearance and use differs somewhat.

Study the information returned to you on the screen, and develop a feel for how each appears. Ideally, you will be able to select the proper utility to troubleshoot the problem, given its symptoms. Once you've used the appropriate tool, you'll be able to interpret the information correctly.

**Software
Exploration**

PROCEDURE

Most TCP/IP utilities are run from a command-line screen, which is the command prompt on client computers.

1. Navigate the *Start/Programs/Accessories* path and select the **Command Prompt** option.

ARP is a convention used to map IP addresses to physical MAC addresses. Not only is it a tool available for your use, ARP is also a sophisticated address resolution protocol that's routinely used between routers. At the LAN and client level, the resolution maps are contained in clients or servers and include addresses between machines.

2. From a client machine that's connected to the Internet, enter (at the DOS screen) **arp**.

Your screen will show the commands available for use with ARP. It's a useful tool for examining the contents of ARP caches on either the client or the server station.

3. At the command prompt, enter **arp -a**, and the screen will return information similar to Figure 33-1.

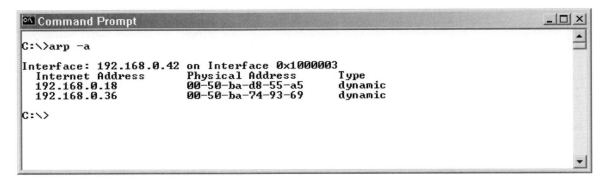

Figure 33-1: ARP Utility is Used to Identify Addressing Information

The following describes the purpose of the fields.

- **INTERFACE**: This is the IP of the machine running the ARP utility.
- **INTERNET ADDRESS**: This is the address of a server that the machine is connected to. The first address is the latest connection.
- **PHYSICAL ADDRESS**: This is the MAC address of the corresponding IP.
- **TYPE**: This is the type of connection from local machine to server, and may be Dynamic or Static.

In addition to querying the ARP cache, entries may be added to it with the **-s** command, or deleted from it with the **-d** command. The **hostname** command returns the name of the system on which the command is executed.

4. At the command prompt from the NT server, enter **hostname**.

*NOTE: The name displayed on your screen was entered when the NOS (NT, for example) was set up. It refers to the network server. **Ipconfig** is a utility that tells you addressing information for the system you are currently connected to.*

5. At the command prompt from a client, enter **ipconfig /all**.

The window should look similar to Figure 33-2.

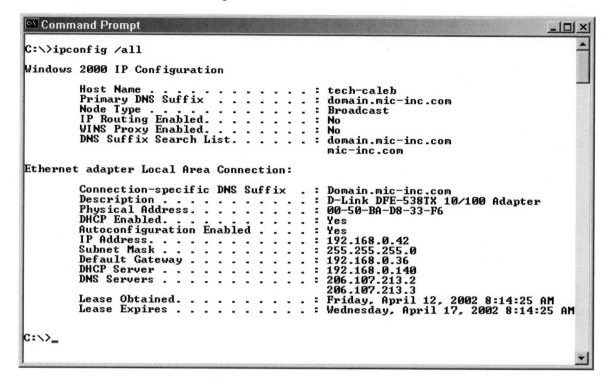

```
Command Prompt                                                          _ □ ×

C:\>ipconfig /all

Windows 2000 IP Configuration

        Host Name . . . . . . . . . . . . : tech-caleb
        Primary DNS Suffix  . . . . . . . : domain.mic-inc.com
        Node Type . . . . . . . . . . . . : Broadcast
        IP Routing Enabled. . . . . . . . : No
        WINS Proxy Enabled. . . . . . . . : No
        DNS Suffix Search List. . . . . . : domain.mic-inc.com
                                            mic-inc.com

Ethernet adapter Local Area Connection:

        Connection-specific DNS Suffix  . : Domain.mic-inc.com
        Description . . . . . . . . . . . : D-Link DFE-538TX 10/100 Adapter
        Physical Address. . . . . . . . . : 00-50-BA-D8-33-F6
        DHCP Enabled. . . . . . . . . . . : Yes
        Autoconfiguration Enabled . . . . : Yes
        IP Address. . . . . . . . . . . . : 192.168.0.42
        Subnet Mask . . . . . . . . . . . : 255.255.255.0
        Default Gateway . . . . . . . . . : 192.168.0.36
        DHCP Server . . . . . . . . . . . : 192.168.0.140
        DNS Servers . . . . . . . . . . . : 206.107.213.2
                                            206.107.213.3
        Lease Obtained. . . . . . . . . . : Friday, April 12, 2002 8:14:25 AM
        Lease Expires . . . . . . . . . . : Wednesday, April 17, 2002 8:14:25 AM

C:\>_
```

Figure 33-2: Ipconfig/all is Used to Return IP Address Information

Notice that the information is separated into two categories—server and client (taken from the network interface card installed in the client computer).

In the network listings, you should see the name of the host (server) that the client machine connects with, along with any pertinent status information about the session between the client and the server. In the client listings, notice that the IP address of the client computer is listed in hexadecimal format, along with the subnet mask and default gateway—if one is used. Using ipconfig is an easy way to retrieve IP addresses.

6. For a quick overview of the configuration, enter **ipconfig**.

This returns the same information as above, but in abbreviated form.

The **nbtstat** (NetBIOS over a TCP connection) tool is used with Windows machines to provide information about the remote connection. When entered, it shows information about network names and their corresponding IP address.

7. From the command prompt, type **nbtstat**.

The screen will fill with commands available with the tool.

8. At the command prompt, type **net view \\(your server name)**.

9. Type **nbtstat -s** to list the sessions table with destination IP addresses. The window should look similar to Figure 33-3.

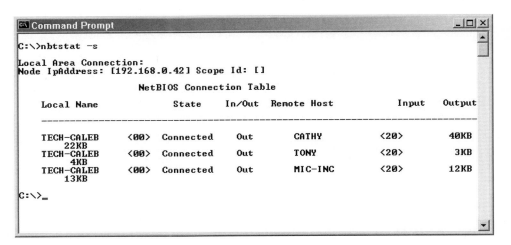

Figure 33-3: nbtstat -s

For "your server name", enter the actual name of the server your machine is connected to. An example of net view is shown in Figure 33-4. As you can see, the list includes all share devices associated with the machine name.

```
Command Prompt                                                    _ □ ×

C:\>net view \\mic-inc
Shared resources at \\mic-inc


Share name     Type        Used as   Comment
-------------------------------------------------------------------------
Bradon         Disk
clt-inst       Disk
Database       Disk
Evan's My Documents
               Disk
HPLaserJ       Print                 HP LaserJet 1100 <MS>
Installation Files
               Disk                  Program Installation Files
Jill's backup
               Disk
Lisa's Backups
               Disk
Marsales       Disk
Mike Mail PST
               Disk
MP3's          Disk
NETLOGON       Disk                  Logon server share
Paul's My Documents
               Disk
Profiles       Disk
Stuart         Disk
SYSVOL         Disk                  Logon server share
VPHOME         Disk                  Norton AntiVirus
VPLOGON        Disk                  Norton AntiVirus
WinRoute Pro Disk
The command completed successfully.


C:\>_
```

Figure 33-4: Devices Shared with the Server can be Shown with the NBTSTAT Tool, Net View

10. At the command prompt, type **nbtstat -c**.

This displays the IP address of the machine specified in the step above, as long as it's in the machine cache. The value of this is that it's much more common to refer to network resources by their name, rather than by their IP address. However, it's the address that's used to locate the device when information is sent to it; consequently, it's the IP that will be needed when troubleshooting.

Netstat is a tool used to display all current Network layer connections. This means you'll see TCP/IP or UDP protocols that are active at the time the tool is used. Netstat lists the network connections.

11. At the command prompt, type **netstat ?**.

The screen will show all of the commands used with the netstat tool. The following command will display all connections on the server that your machine is connected to.

12. At the command prompt, type **netstat -r**.

The display lists all connections, and shows which are active at the time the utility is run. Another interesting application of NETSTAT is to view statistics related to the interface of your machine to the network.

13. At the command prompt, type **netstat -e**.

The information listed will show the number of bytes received and transmitted, the type of packets, and, of particular interest, the number of errors generated. An example of netstat -e is presented in Figure 33-5.

```
Command Prompt                                              _ |□| x|
C:\>netstat -e
Interface Statistics

                          Received              Sent

Bytes                     38953084          54617995
Unicast packets              58358             67767
Non-unicast packets           4080               302
Discards                         0                 0
Errors                           0                 0
Unknown protocols            11808

C:\>_
```

Figure 33-3: NETSTAT -e Shows Statistical Information About the Current Session

Suppose that you suspect a client of having a faulty network interface card. The exercise above will list any errors that occurred at the client. Adding a number at the end of the above command is optional. For example, adding " 5" at the end of the command will update the listing every 5 seconds.

Ping is a tool used to check the status of a connection. An echo packet is sent to a specified address and returned to your machine, if the specified address is active. If it's not, you'll receive a message stating that the transaction has timed-out. The effect of the ping tool is similar to measuring continuity with an ohmmeter. It checks to see if two network devices are connected. If they are, an echo is returned to the sending station. If they aren't, the ping will time-out.

14. To initiate ping, enter **ping**.

The screen will list all of the commands that are used with the tool.

15. At the command prompt, type **ping (the IP of the local server you're connected to)**.

16. If you can't remember the IP of the local server, use one of the tools you've already become familiar with to retrieve the IP.

As you can see from the reply, the connection from your machine to the server is working. It's time to ping an IP you're not connected to.

17. At the command prompt, type **ping 123.456.789.123**.

NOTE: After a short wait, you should receive the Request timed out message.

What's happened is that the message couldn't find a destination at the specified address, and after a while was discarded. The notation "TTL" stands for Time To Live, which is a field in the IP header. It's an instruction to any devices receiving the packet to discard it if the time specified in the field is exceeded.

Tracert allows you to see the path to an address. When an IP address is specified, tracert lists the number of hops to the destination along with the IP addresses of each router along the way. You can specify the number of hops to the destination to determine the most efficient route. It's also a good tool to use to determine whether a problem lies at the remote address, or is within the route to the destination.

For example, assume you ping a remote server, but don't receive a response. The question then becomes: Is the problem at the destination, or at one of the routers along the way? The way to pinpoint the problem is to connect to the router that is at the end of the list, then try to connect to the destination from there. If you can't, the problem most likely lies at that router.

18. To initiate tracert, type **tracert**.

The screen will show all of the tracert commands.

19. From a client connected to the Internet, type **tracert -h 192.31.7.130**.

This will show the path to the CISCO site. Your screen will show the number of hops to the site from your location, along with the time from hop to hop. An example is shown in Figure 33-6.

```
Command Prompt                                                    _ □ ×

C:\>tracert cio-sys.cisco.com

Tracing route to cio-sys.cisco.com [198.133.219.34]
over a maximum of 30 hops:

  1     41 ms     40 ms     30 ms  ds11-01.dynacom.net [206.159.132.129]
  2     30 ms     30 ms     40 ms  ken-3640.dynacom.net [206.107.213.1]
  3    240 ms    240 ms    181 ms  sl-gw2-sea-5-4.sprintlink.net [144.228.94.197]
  4     60 ms     50 ms     60 ms  sl-bb20-sea-2-0.sprintlink.net [144.232.6.25]
  5     90 ms     50 ms     60 ms  sl-bb20-tac-9-0.sprintlink.net [144.232.18.41]
  6     70 ms     90 ms     71 ms  sl-bb20-sj-5-2.sprintlink.net [144.232.9.213]
  7     70 ms     80 ms     70 ms  sl-gw11-sj-9-0.sprintlink.net [144.232.3.138]
  8     60 ms     50 ms     70 ms  sl-ciscopsn2-11-0-0.sprintlink.net [144.228.44.1
4]
  9     70 ms     70 ms     60 ms  sjck-dirty-gw1.cisco.com [128.107.239.5]
 10    100 ms     70 ms     61 ms  sjck-sdf-ciod-gw2.cisco.com [128.107.239.110]
 11    180 ms     90 ms    111 ms  cio-sys.cisco.com [198.133.219.34]

Trace complete.

C:\>
```

Figure 33-4: Tracert Shows the Number of Hops to a Designated IP Address

Tracert is more appropriate in a wide area environment. You can try using it while connected to the Internet by specifying well-known IP addresses, such as those to Microsoft or Netscape.

Telnet is a service that allows you to "telephone-net" into another computer. The original idea was that if you were in Atlanta, and needed access to information in a computer in Dallas, you could telnet into it. The information was presented on your terminal screen just as if you were sitting in Dallas at a terminal connected directly to the Dallas computer. Telnet remains, but its application is specialized and limited primarily to setting up and troubleshooting networks.

A telnet screen can be invoked from the command prompt by typing telnet. Once you enter it, a telnet terminal emulation screen opens and you must enter the IP address of the computer you want to dial into. Figure 33-7 shows a telnet screen from a Windows NT client.

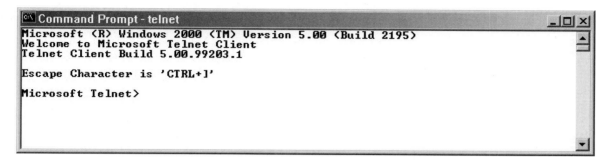

Figure 33-5: Telnet is Used for a Remote Connection

FTP (File Transfer Protocol) is a means of downloading files to your computer; or uploading them from your computer to an FTP site. Like e-mail, FTP retains a distinct structure, probably because it too was introduced early in the formation of the Internet. The widest application of FTP is for downloading software or software enhancements. For example, many vendors have a download section at their web site. If you've bought a product from a vendor in the past, you can use their web site to download the latest revision of the software that's used in the product. Patches, upgrades, or fixes to problems are routinely posted at a company's download area.

It's also a very useful troubleshooting tool for TCP/IP because if a file can be sent or received, it must be working. Once the file transfer has taken place, you can use the data from the transaction to evaluate the quality of the transfer.

To begin an FTP session, you enter **ftp** at the command prompt. The prompt then changes to an FTP prompt (FTP). Next, you enter the address—typically a domain-like name as used on the Internet.

LAB QUESTIONS

1. What is the purpose of PING?
2. What is the purpose of IPCONFIG?
3. What is the purpose of NETSTAT?
4. What is the purpose of TRACERT?
5. What is the purpose of NBTSTAT?

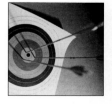

Feedback

Additional Connectivity Topics

OBJECTIVES

1. Experiment with subnet mask information.
2. Establish IP Filtering.
3. Use an Incorrect Protocol.
4. Experiment with FTP services.
5. View Remote Error Events.

Software Exploration

RESOURCES

1. Network+ Certification Training Guide
2. Windows 2000 Professional Installation CD
3. Network Access to your partner's workstation

DISCUSSION

There are many problems that could arise when establishing network connectivity. Various incorrect TCP/IP settings could be the source of problems. Sometimes the protocol itself is not present on the workstation. It is possible to view some errors remotely to troubleshoot connectivity problems. This and other issues will be addressed in this lab.

NOTE: This procedure assumes that you are using statically assigned IP addressing information.

PROCEDURE

1. From the Windows 2000 desktop, right-click on **My Network Places** and click on **Properties**.

2. Right-click on **Local Area Connection** and click on **Properties**.

Software Exploration

3. Select **Internet Protocol (TCP/IP)** and click on **Properties**.

4. Your IP address for a class C network is likely in the form of "192.X.X.X". Verify that the last number is less than 252. If not, change it to an available number. Ask your instructor if you are not sure what is available.

5. Record the new address in Table 34-1.

6. The subnet mask, by default, is set to "255.255.255.0". Change it to "255.255.255.252".

7. Click on **OK** for both windows that are opened; the changes will be applied.

8. Open a command prompt by clicking on **Start/Run** and entering **cmd**.

9. As you have done in previous procedures, ping your partner's computer next to you. Record the results in Table 34-2.

10. Close the command prompt and open the **TCP/IP Properties** window as before.

11. Leave the subnet the same and change the last number of your IP address to a number greater than or equal to 252.

12. Save the changes and try pinging your partner's computer again. Record the results in Table 34-3.

13. Close the command prompt and open the **TCP/IP Properties** window as before.

14. Change the **IP Address** and **Subnet mask** back to their original settings (before you made any changes).

15. Click on **OK** to both Windows to save the settings.

16. We will now experiment with TCP/IP Filtering. Enter the **Internet Protocol (TCP/IP) Properties** window as before.

17. Click on the **Advanced** button.

18. Click on the **Options** Tab and select **TCP/IP Filtering**.

19. Click on the **Properties** button. You will see a window similar to Figure 34-1.

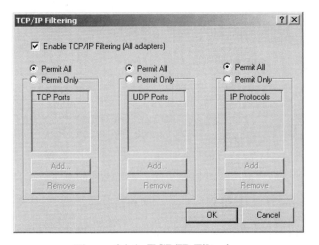

Figure 34-1: TCP/IP Filtering

20. In the leftmost field, TCP Ports, click on the **Permit Only** radio button. Do not add any ports to the list. Click on **OK** for the window.

21. Click on **OK** for all the other windows to save the changes. You will be prompted to restart the computer. Click on **Yes** to do so.

22. After your partner at the computer next to you has also enabled TCP/IP Filtering, enter the command prompt and ping their computer.

23. Record the results in Table 34-4.

24. Now, type **net view IPADDRESS**, where IPADDRESS is the IP of the computer next to you.

25. Record the results in Table 34-5.

26. Close the command prompt and navigate to **TCP/IP Filtering Properties** as before.

27. Change the TCP Ports field radio button to its previous setting, **Permit All**.

28. To save the settings, click on **OK** to all the windows and restart the computer when prompted.

29. After both computers have restarted, enter the command prompt as before.

30. As before, type **net view IPADDRESS**. Record the results in Table 34-6.

31. Close all windows.

32. We will now see an error with incorrect protocols. Enter the **Local Area Connection Properties** window as before.

33. Remove TCP/IP by selecting **Internet Protocol (TCP/IP)** and clicking on the **Uninstall** button. You will see a warning window similar to Figure 34-2.

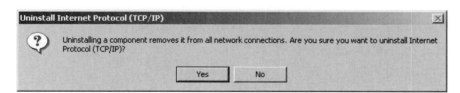

Figure 34-2: Uninstall Warning

34. Click on **Yes** to the warning. When prompted to restart the computer click on **No**.

35. We will now install another protocol. Click on the **Install** button, select **Protocol**, and click on **Add**.

36. Select the **AppleTalk Protocol** and click on **OK**.

37. Close the **Local Area Connection Properties** and restart the computer.

38. After the computer has restarted, open a command prompt and type **ping IPADDRESS**, where IPADDRESS is any IP address available.

39. Record the error in Table 34-7.

40. Close the command prompt and open Internet Explorer.

41. Record the error in Table 34-7.

42. Open the **Local Area Connection Properties** window as before.

43. As you have done before, uninstall the **AppleTalk Protocol** and install **Internet Protocol (TCP/IP)**.

44. Configure TCP/IP to its original configuration. Restart the computer if necessary.

45. IIS now needs to be installed on the computer to enable FTP services. Click on **Start/Settings/Control Panel** and select **Add/Remove Programs**.

46. Click on **Add/Remove Windows Components**. Select **Internet Information Services (IIS)** by placing a check mark next to it and click on **Next**.

47. Insert the Windows 2000 CD when prompted and click on **OK**.

48. Click on **Finish** after IIS is installed and close the **Add/Remove Programs** window.

49. From Control Panel, open **Administrative Tools/Event Viewer**.

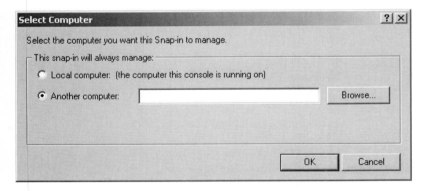

Figure 34-3: Connect to Remote Event Viewer

50. Right-click on the **Event Viewer** root and select **Connect to another computer**. You will see a window similar to Figure 34-3.

51. Enter the UNC name of your partner's computer or browse to locate the computer and click on **OK**.

52. Click on the **System** node. You will see a list of warning, error, and information alerts in the right-hand window pane.

53. With Event Viewer still active, open a command prompt.

54. Type **ftp xxx.xxx.xxx.xxx**, where xxx is the IP address of your partner's computer.

55. Enter a false username and password when prompted. The window will look similar to Figure 34-4.

```
C:\WINNT\System32\cmd.exe - ftp 192.168.0.46
Microsoft Windows 2000 [Version 5.00.2195]
(C) Copyright 1985-2000 Microsoft Corp.

C:\>ftp 192.168.0.46
Connected to 192.168.0.46.
220 caleb2000 Microsoft FTP Service (Version 5.0).
User (192.168.0.46:(none)): bogus
331 Password required for bogus.
Password:
530 User bogus cannot log in.
Login failed.
ftp> _
```

Figure 34-4: FTP Error

56. Now, switch tasks to the Event Viewer that is viewing your partner's computer. You will see a window similar to Figure 34-5.

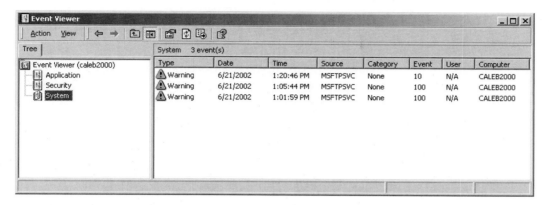

Figure 34-5: Event Viewer

57. Double-click on the latest warning that appears. Record the description of the warning in Table 34-8.

58. Close all windows and shut down the computer.

TABLES

Table 34-1: IP Address

Table 34-2: Ping Results

Table 34-3: Ping Results

Table 34-4: Ping Results

Table 34-5: Net View Results

Table 34-6: Net View Results

Table 34-7: Missing Protocol Errors

Ping	
Internet Explorer	

Table 34-8: Warning Description

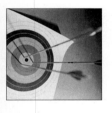

Feedback

LAB QUESTIONS

1. What effect does the subnet mask have on accessibility?
2. How could you permit only e-mail and FTP access to your computer?
3. Does the default IIS FTP site run by default?